Canine Agility and
the Meaning of Excellence

"Dogs in Our World" Series

Canine Crania: Your Dog's Head and Why It Looks That Way
(Bryan D. Cummins with Kaelyn Racine, 2024)

*The Peace Puppy: A Memoir of Caregiving
and Canine Solace* (Susan Hartzler, 2024)

My Broken Dog: Living with a Handicapped Pet
(Sandy Kubillus, 2024)

Canine Agility and the Meaning of Excellence
(Beth A. Dixon, 2024)

We Saved Each Other (Christopher Dale, 2024)

*Police Dogs of Trinidad and Tobago:
A 70-Year History* (Debbie Jacob, 2024)

*The Force-Free Dilemma: Truth and Myths
in Modern Dog Training* (Nicola Ferguson, 2024)

*Dogs of the Railways: Canine Guardians, Companions
and Mascots Since the 19th Century* (Jill Lenk Schilp, 2023)

Horror Dogs: Man's Best Friend as Movie Monster
(Brian Patrick Duggan, 2023)

*I Know Your Dog Is a Good Dog: A Trainer's Insights on Reactive,
Aggressive or Anxious Behavior* (Linda Scroggins, 2023)

*The Most Painful Choice: A Dog Owner's Story
of Behavioral Euthanasia* (Beth Miller, 2023)

Your Service Dog and You: A Practical Guide (Nicola Ferguson, 2023)

*Dog of the Decade: Breed Trends and What They Mean
in America* (Deborah Thompson, 2022)

*Laboratory Dogs Rescued: From Test Subjects
to Beloved Companions* (Ellie Hansen, 2022)

*Beware of Dog: How Media Portrays
the Aggressive Canine* (Melissa Crawley, 2021)

*I'm Not Single, I Have a Dog: Dating Tales
from the Bark Side* (Susan Hartzler, 2021)

*Dogs in Health Care: Pioneering Animal-Human
Partnerships* (Jill Lenk Schilp, 2019)

*General Custer, Libbie Custer and Their Dogs:
A Passion for Hounds, from the Civil War to Little Bighorn*
(Brian Patrick Duggan, 2019)

*Dog's Best Friend: Will Judy, Founder of National Dog Week
and* Dog World *Publisher* (Lisa Begin-Kruysman, 2014)

*Man Writes Dog: Canine Themes in Literature,
Law and Folklore* (William Farina, 2014)

*Saluki: The Desert Hound and the English Travelers
Who Brought It to the West* (Brian Patrick Duggan, 2009)

Canine Agility and the Meaning of Excellence

Formulating an Ethical Approach

BETH A. DIXON

DOGS IN OUR WORLD
Series Editor Brian Patrick Duggan

McFarland & Company, Inc., Publishers
Jefferson, North Carolina

Library of Congress Cataloguing-in-Publication Data

Names: Dixon, B. A. (Beth A.), 1957– author
Title: Canine agility and the meaning of excellence : formulating an ethical approach / Beth A. Dixon.
Description: Jefferson, North Carolina : McFarland & Company, Inc., Publishers, 2024 | Series: Dogs in our world | Includes bibliographical references and index.
Identifiers: LCCN 2024031990 | ISBN 9781476653921 ebook ∞
ISBN 9781476694092 paperback
Subjects: LCSH: Dogs—Agility trials | Dogs—Training—Moral and ethical aspects
Classification: LCC SF425.4 .D58 2024 | DDC 636.7—dc23
LC record available at https://lccn.loc.gov/2024031990

British Library cataloguing data are available
**ISBN (print) 978-1-4766-9409-2
ISBN (ebook) 978-1-4766-5392-1**

© 2024 Beth A. Dixon. All rights reserved

No part of this book may be reproduced or transmitted in any form or by any means, electronic or mechanical, including photocopying or recording, or by any information storage and retrieval system, without permission in writing from the publisher.

Front cover image: Robin Magee's youngest dog, Sequence, shows his commitment to a jump. Northern Magic Agility Dogs (NOMAD) U.K.I. Trial in Colchester, Vermont, July 2023 (photograph by Donna Lineman).

Printed in the United States of America

*McFarland & Company, Inc., Publishers
Box 611, Jefferson, North Carolina 28640
www.mcfarlandpub.com*

*In memory of the dogs
who taught us about agility:*

*Caro (1995–2007)
Rugby (2002–2013)
Gryffin (2007–2023)
Thisby (2014–2023)
Phoebe (2003–2016)
Ziva (2010–2022)
Sasha (1997–2011)
Kaden (2001–2010)
Neeps (2000–2011)
Nash (2008–2019)
Shay (1999–2010)
Sidney (1999–2010)
Evan (2003–2020)
Saucony (2008–2021)
Sprint (2010–2017)*

Table of Contents

Acknowledgments	xi
Preface	1
Introduction	3
What Is This Book About?	6
Why Stories?	10
One. The Problem of Excellence	13
The Story of Dusty	13
Moral Character and Excellence	18
Maggie's Online Trials	19
Some Questions About Exceptional Performance	24
Why Agility?	25
Agility as Hobby	27
Agility Organizations	28
Training Excellence	28
Telling Stories	29
Introducing Sue Hall	29
Summary	32
Two. Exceptional Performance	35
What Is a Qualifying Run?	36
Tiny, Beautiful Moments	42
Skills	44
When Do We Cheer, and for Whom?	45
What Does Luck Have to Do with It?	48
"Matters of Fortune"	50
Introducing Sue Pietricola	52
What Does Excellence in Agility Look Like?	53
Summary	54
Three. Agility as Play	57
Agility Is Not Just Something We Do on the Side	57

Table of Contents

Moral Virtues	62
Playing Agility	65
What Is Play?	68
Excellent Play	70
Amateurs Play, Professionals Excel	71
Introducing JoLee Yeddo	72
Summary	77

Four. Agility as Hobby — 80

Recreation	81
"The Gentle Pursuit of a Modest Competence"	85
What Is a Hobby?	86
The Amateur Hour	89
The Core of Excellence	90
An Objection	91
Does Your Dog Have a Hobby?	94
Introducing Ann Benjamin and Jodi Pangman	95
Summary	99

Five. The Internal Goods of Agility — 101

Internal and External Rewards	102
What Is a Practice?	104
The Relational Values of Agility	107
Who Displays Excellence?	109
Do Agility Institutions Corrupt?	114
Introducing Diane Fyfe	117
Summary	121

Six. Training Excellence — 123

A Great Dog	124
Training Capability	126
Respect	128
Trust	131
Communication	135
Introducing Robin Magee	138
Summary	144

Seven. How to Tell a Story About Excellence — 145

Intelligible Behavior	146
Narrative Arc	147
Who Am I?	149
The Explanatory Value of Stories	152
The Role of Fancy	155
The Ethical Value of Stories	159

Table of Contents

"Muster Dogs" 161
Summary 165

Chapter Notes 167

Bibliography 169

Index 173

Acknowledgments

The following people generously agreed to be interviewed for this project: Ann Benjamin, Diane Fyfe, Sue Hall, Robin Magee, Jodi Pangman, Sue Pietricola, and JoLee Yeddo. They gave up their time from work, teaching agility students, retirement activities, training their dogs, competing their dogs, judging agility trials, and spending time with family to answer my questions. The most profound idea that emerged from each person I interviewed is that excellence can be identified almost anywhere in the practice of our sport. For these agility devotees, excellence is not some rarified performance that is an unreachable ideal. Rather, it might be on display in a short sequence of jumps in the practice field, it might be on display in a non-qualifying run at a competition, or it might be on display in a moment of training. Thank you all for your clarity and eloquence. I am endlessly grateful for your contributions.

I have used material here from some previously published works. I thank the publishers for permitting me to use excerpts and revised versions of articles and book chapters. Part of Chapter One includes "Maggie's Online Trials" which was first published by *Clean Run—The Magazine for Dog Agility Enthusiasts*, vol. 26, no. 11 (November 2020), pp. 28–29. Chapter Three includes an excerpt from "Life Lessons: Agility Is Not Just Something We Do on the Side" which was first published by *Clean Run—The Magazine for Dog Agility Enthusiasts*, vol. 26, no. 12 (December 2020), pp. 10–12. Chapter Seven includes an excerpt from one of my earlier published books, *Animals, Emotion, and Morality: Marking the Boundary*, Rowman & Littlefield (2008).

And a huge thank you to those photographers whose professionalism, sense of style, and just basic willingness to help brought this

Acknowledgments

The author's dog, Maggie, attacks the weave poles. Working Australian Shepherd Club of Upstate New York (WASCUNY) Trial at High Goal Farm, April 2021 (photograph by David K. Cerilli).

project to life: David Cerilli, Sue Lezon, Ben Griffith, Donna Lineman, Michelle Osborne, Sue Pietricola, and Shanon Waddingham.

Finally, I could not have finished without the encouragement and philosophical expertise of my husband, Chuck. He can always be counted on to happily read yet another draft of my work, adding his expertise from a lifetime of teaching and writing about philosophy.

Maggie receives the last but not least tribute. She makes me deliriously happy, most of the time.

Preface

This book is a philosophical inquiry about the meaning of excellence in agility. Why does the agility community need such a book? Because no matter how accomplished we are as trainers, students, or competitors, we are all either striving for excellence, realizing excellence, or falling short of it, sometimes by a lot. I venture that we don't always know exactly what we are aiming for when we are striving, realizing, or falling short. And even if some of us do believe that we know what excellence is, it still remains for this preferred definition to be justified and defended. So my contribution to practitioners of the sport is a rather specialized one, and that is to formulate and to argue for what I believe is a credible concept of excellence; I call this the *ethical concept of excellence.*

Excellence has ethical connotations in ancient philosophy, especially, and the concept is ubiquitous in the literature of the philosophy of sport as an idea worth clarifying and analyzing. My ambition is to use these philosophical resources to elucidate the real-world activity of agility. The risk of this kind of project is that the theory will float uselessly above the practical, finding no points of intersection. I've tried hard not to let that happen. But to keep my feet firmly planted in the agility field rather than philosophical abstraction, I've interviewed practitioners themselves about what excellence in agility means. You will hear from members of my weekly agility class, trainers, instructors, fellow competitors, and judges, each of whom possesses a vast amount of expertise and experience. But just to be clear, I am not trying to instruct anyone about *how* to be excellent in agility. Look elsewhere if you are merely interested in enhancing agility performance outcomes. There are plenty of other books, podcasts, online training courses, and videos to choose from. My inspiration

Preface

for this topic did not begin with success, as you will learn. It was born out of moments of failure and frustration. From this vantage point it made sense to ask, "What am I trying to do?" This kind of question usually marks the start line for philosophical inquiry.

Consider that a good friend of mine has recently lost her agility dog, a darling Corgi named Thisby. There are few words to comfort this kind of loss. My own dog, Maggie, suffered a tendon injury. The uncertainty about her sport-fitness left me wondering if she would ever return to agility. Another friend and agility competitor is suffering from physical pain when she runs her dogs. Nothing seems to help, and she is struggling to imagine how she can remain physically active and to continue to participate in this sport. These events make me wonder why it is that we continue to throw our hearts away. We direct so much passion and love into our dogs and dog sports. But we only make ourselves vulnerable when, inevitably, these animals and things that matter most to us are suddenly taken from our lives. Perhaps this plight is what makes us human. We ardently pursue what makes our lives full and rich, what some philosophers call "a good life." But these conditions that satisfy are only contingently available to us. We do not entirely control the presence or absence of those conditions that make a flourishing life. This is what Martha Nussbaum (1986, 20) calls "the fragility of goodness." Imagine that an excellent human life is like a plant that requires the right external conditions in order to flourish and to grow, such as soil, water, and sun. But the plant will wilt or die if these conditions are absent or severely diminished. In this sense flourishing (or human excellence) is fragile, depending as it does on conditions beyond the control of human agency. So when we are robbed of a beloved animal or an activity about which we are passionate, it is natural to acknowledge that any life that is worth living is a vulnerable one, sustained not by necessity or pure strength of will, but by an accidental and temporary grace. What to do when faced with the absence of something so beloved? As Hearne (1994, 98–99) recommends, "Another dog, same breed, right away.... A decade went by between the death of Gunner and the purchase of the new Airedale pup. That was as soon as I could get to it, what with one thing and another."

Introduction

> *This, then, is a sketch of the good; for, presumably, we must draw the outline first, and fill it in later. If the sketch is good, anyone it seems can advance and articulate it, and in such cases time discovers more, or is a good partner in discovery. That is also how the crafts have improved, since anyone can add what is lacking [in the outline]* (Aristotle 1985, 1098a20–25).

Some of my friends and acquaintances who have watched me run Maggie in competitive agility events would be *very* surprised that I am writing about excellence in agility. According to most of these people our performance has fallen quite a bit short of excellent for some time now. So what could I possibly have to say about this exalted quality, a quality that my dog and I rarely, if ever, exhibit? Contrary to popular opinion, being eliminated from class after class has given me a unique perspective about what excellence is. And being a philosopher, I am now motivated and keenly interested in exploring the *concept* of excellence in agility from the many possible candidate definitions to the various ways in which dogs and handlers might exemplify this concept. Success in a particular sport does not necessarily guarantee insight about the nature of success. But failing to achieve success can indeed trigger some deep reflection about how and why these failures occur. Or maybe the nature of success and the "excellence" of this sport is more complex and less obvious than everyone seems to think.

I've studied the course map and I've walked the course, looking at angles, turns, and approaches. I've thought about how fast Maggie will be coming out of the tunnel and where I want to be in order to

Introduction

tell her in advance that we will be curling left to an obstacle. I want her on my right side as she comes barreling out. I'm trying to organize a million reminders about my hands (don't wave them around), my shoulders and feet (where they point), and my verbal cue "out" at just the right moment so Maggie knows to move away from me on a bending line. And I tell myself, "Just keep your eyes on her." Staying connected is the most important thing that I will try to remember. Maggie sometimes misses an obstacle to follow me if I'm not looking at her, even though I cue it and it is right in front of her! This is not obstinacy or disobedience. She just wants and needs to be connected with me as we run.

But in a moment none of this planning and rehearsing matters. By the time I line her up at the start line, tell her to "stay," and run out to the first jump, she has already broken her start. In her excitement, she herself has decided that it is time to go. I wasn't ready, and she piles into me, creating a jumble of legs and jump bars. I take her back to the start line, and with much barking and scooting around, I eventually line her up again. But we have already been eliminated for this class. And the clock is ticking. We have only 25 seconds to do a few jumps before we are whistled out of the ring.

Fast forward to another trial and another class. As before I learn the course and walk it to form a plan for handling the twists and turns of this Jumper course. Again, we don't even start. This time I sit Maggie down in front of the first jump and take off her leash to throw behind me. She barks, sidles out of reach, and then grabs her leash on the ground and carries it around, bouncing and careening near me, but not too close. She looks absolutely joyous. But in that moment I regard her as a *delinquent*. My repeated commands to "come" don't make a bit of difference. Eventually I get her under control and peek at the judge. "I guess that's our time," I say regretfully. All I hear is "Thank you" as we slink out of the ring.

I could go on and on about trials where we didn't even start to run a course, and those many, many eliminations we amassed during the spring, summer, and fall of 2021. But I think you get the idea. The main reason for revisiting these painful episodes is to ask a question that is not so easy for me to answer: Why am I doing this? As I write this I have withdrawn from an A.K.C. trial for which I signed up and

Introduction

paid. I decided to pause the competitive trialing until I could provide an honest answer to this basic question. One thing I know is that right now, trialing is not fun for me. And I'm not sure about Maggie.

For me the qualifying run is a seduction. Not very long ago it came to stand for disappointment, despair, shame, and the real possibility that I would quit doing competitive agility altogether. I didn't start trialing with a plan to accumulate points, titles, and Facebook cheers. I started by just being happy that Maggie did not jump all over the judge and ring crew. Over time she got focused and serious about the ring, and we sailed through the rather easy courses, accumulating ribbons and titles. Then everything changed. We have been eliminated from so many classes that I can't even keep track of them. It's just a blur of whistles, bells, and "Thank you's" (please leave the ring now). So I have felt pretty low and unaccomplished for a long time now. I've been seeking exceptional performance, and not even getting close.

For those of us who are earnest but merely competent practitioners of the sport, exceptional performance is not a rational quest but it persists as an aspirational ideal. That is the tragic part of the dilemma I face and, perhaps, others do as well. We want to be elite handlers with elite performance dogs because this rarefied standard of excellence is one we have internalized and quietly or implicitly endorsed. But for many of us there are too many obstacles that impede our successful accomplishment of this goal. We are older or less agile handlers. We have less time or money to train. We may not have our own agility fields in which to practice. Maybe we have a dog who is over-aroused and difficult to run. Or maybe we have an older or slow dog who must be constantly urged to run at all. The standard ways of responding to our often frustrated practice of the sport of agility is to be happy when your friends succeed, be happy with a good start-line stay or a good sequence of jumps, be happy with the relationship you have with your dog, be satisfied training your dog at a trial or at home, enjoy the community of agility enthusiasts, or be mindful that this is a hard sport. These are all comforting attitudes to adopt. But they are (psychologically) poor substitutes for the triumph one feels from accomplishing fast, clean qualifying runs. It's like throwing crumbs to someone who hungers for a different kind

Introduction

of success. I believe the main problem is that by implicitly endorsing a standard of excellence that we can rarely meet, we negatively shape what it is like to participate in the sport of agility. If I *usually* fall short of an expected standard, then I will *usually* feel frustrated, unsatisfied, or discouraged. And we might expect that in one way or another this attitude will translate into a disheartened attitude toward my dog, who is trying so hard to please me.

What Is This Book About?

The main question I explore, "What is excellence in agility?" should be of interest to all practitioners of the sport. This includes amateurs like myself who occasionally enter competitive trials, those people who go to an agility class once or twice a week but never compete, and trainers who teach agility classes and seminars as well as elite handlers and their highly trained performance dogs who chase points and titles and who aspire to become eligible for national or international competitions. Additionally, there are many people who just play with their dogs using agility equipment set up in their backyards. It seems to me that all practitioners of agility are trying to achieve excellence, whatever that turns out to be. But one can't help noticing that excellence in the practice ring may look very different from excellence in the competitive trial setting. Excellence for a new handler and her novice dog may manifest in a completely different way from what more experienced agility teams realize. And what about the backyard enthusiast? Doesn't she aspire to excellence in the activity too? The main idea I advance here is perhaps more controversial. I argue that there is a univocal concept of excellence that ranges over all of these different contexts of agility. I call this the *ethical concept of excellence.*

For agility practitioners I believe there is a crucial need to formulate a single concept of excellence since without one there is a lack of clarity about what we are trying to achieve when we undertake this sport with our dogs. It might turn out that almost anything will count as excellent or nothing will count, only because we have not clarified the aspirational ideal. But worse and,

Introduction

The author's dog, Maggie, is poised at the peak of the A-frame. Southern Adirondack Agility Club (SAAC) Trial at High Goal Farm, April 2020 (photograph by David K. Cerilli).

tragically, we may unreflectingly import a concept of excellence into our practice of the sport that we cannot reasonably satisfy. In this case we are denied the pleasure and satisfaction of doing the activity well. As a result, achieving excellence may become so rarified that we are typically disappointed in ourselves and our dogs. The philosophical and real-world examination of the concept of excellence that I undertake here addresses this crucial omission in how we understand and practice the sport of agility.

As practitioners of the sport we think about what we are doing and why. We evaluate successes and failures in the practice field and at competitions, and we deliberate about the quality of life for ourselves as handlers as well as for our dogs. In other words, we reason and reflect about the practice of agility and our participation in it. This makes agility, as well as other sports, ripe for philosophical analysis. Philosophical inquiry finds its natural home in settings where there are open-ended concepts at work and when it is

Introduction

clear that these concepts apply to the world with consequences. The meaning of "excellence" is not exhausted by a dictionary definition. The concept invites us to explore what it means and how it applies in particular contexts. One concern I have is that practitioners of agility will invariably measure their own success by a kind of default definition of excellence: a display of perfect skills or perfect runs. Instead we should reevaluate the idea that excellence is essentially connected to performance, not because it allows the poor performers among us to feel better, but because the ethical concept that I recommend brings us closer to the heart and soul of our sport. Let me explain further.

I play the flute, but I am not a professional. I am an intermediate player who, at one time, practiced about four to five times a week. Sometimes the tone sounds good to me in the lower octaves, although the high notes are not always so clear. I try to play with expression but my lack of lung power interferes with phrasing. Sometimes I attempt rather fast passages but invariably get my fingers tangled up. So I repeat the same several measures to get it right, or just better. It is reasonable to describe my flute playing practice as striving for excellence. After all, I am not trying to be a poor player or even an average player. But what standard of excellence applies in this context? By some professional musical standard I fall far short of excellence. For example, it would be laughable to audition for a seat in an orchestra or audition to be admitted to Julliard! But why is *professional* musicianship the standard of excellence that applies in this context? I am not just randomly hitting notes and blowing through the mouthpiece. I am trying to do something that approximates what the professional musician does. We have something in common. But it seems uncharitable to say that I will fail to achieve excellence in my playing because I will never play as expertly as world-class flute players. In other words, a standard of excellence should function in a way that is aspirational. It should guide and inspire me to do better, whether it is playing the flute or practicing agility. But it should not operate as an ideal that is rarely, if ever, realized. The solution is the same for both of these problems, flute-playing and practicing agility. It is to analyze the concept of excellence

Introduction

itself. In the case of agility I argue for a "best practices" definition that profiles the internal goods specific to the sport and the relational values that connect handlers with their dogs.

A thorough inquiry invites us to explore reasonable answers to the question "What is excellence in agility?" Here are a few possible answers that deserve closer examination. Excellence in agility is

- exceptional performance;
- a qualifying run, a title, or a championship earned at a competitive event;
- a display of skill by a handler and her dog;
- playing with your dog in an agility ring;
- just getting better, inch by inch;
- realizing the internal rewards of the sport as opposed to the external rewards of the sport; and
- realizing the relational values that connect handlers and their dogs.

Each candidate answer to the main question is itself conceptually complex. For example, we will want to know what exceptional performance is, what the relevant agility skills are, and who can achieve these. What does it mean to get better at a sport like agility? What are the internal rewards of agility activity? And what is the contrast or tension between the internal rewards and the external rewards of the sport? Finally, what are relational values? And why are these central to the practice of agility? Each topic has a point of intersection with some related philosophical ideas that are introduced simply and explained. The philosophical literature ranges over the subject areas of ethics and animals, theoretical ethics, and the philosophy of sport. My aim is not merely to survey the landscape of answers to the main question but to argue for a *plausible* answer. So the methodology is to first present some problems about the concept of excellence in Chapter One. Then I critically evaluate possible solutions to these problems in Chapters Two and Three. Finally, I present and explain my own position about the meaning of excellence in Chapters Four, Five, and Six. By my way of thinking it is not just elite agility practitioners who can realize excellence. Nor do I believe that everyone is excellent. This relativistic position cannot be correct if there

Introduction

exist any criteria whatsoever for realizing excellence. My own view is somewhere in between. There are indeed some conditions that must be satisfied in order to realize ethical excellence. This position allows that even novice handlers and their novice dogs can be excellent in this sense. It is also possible that a winning competitive agility team may fail to realize ethical excellence, although I prefer not to imagine what that would look like.

Why Stories?

My inquiry about excellence is populated by stories about agility. The story is like a lens that magnifies the relevant details about what it means to aspire to excellence, to fall short of excellence, or to realize excellence in a sport. I sometimes include vignettes about my own dog, Maggie, to illustrate the main idea of a chapter. But to explore a topic more thoroughly I also include interviews with practitioners of agility. These are short dialogues with trainers and instructors, agility classmates, judges, and friends that I have made at competitions and in the practice field. I also profile memoirs, documentary films, and fiction about the practice of agility to reveal real-world obstacles as well as examples of success in aspiring to excellence. The main purpose of storytelling is to illustrate the concrete details about what it means to undertake a sport like this, together with a dog. A story can reveal what things look like from the inside point of view, the emotional center of the activity itself, accompanied by all of the desires, pleasures, hopes, fears, or disappointments that we experience when we invest so much passion into an activity. Think of these narratives as a way to envision how it feels to struggle and fail, to struggle and succeed, to revise one's goals, and to admit mistakes. In other words, these stories are entries to an "emotional education" about our sport. Nussbaum (1990, 160) describes this kind of illustrative strategy as "getting the tip."

> Progress comes not from the teaching of an abstract law but by leading the friend, or child, or loved one—by a word, by a story, by an image—to see some new aspect of the concrete case at hand, to see it as this or that.

Introduction

Giving a "tip" is to give a gentle hint about how one might see. The "tip," here, is given not in words at all but in a sudden show of feeling. It is concrete, and it prompts the recognition of the concrete.

I leave the reader with some practical advice about how to give a "tip." In Chapter Seven I formulate five recommendations for how to tell a story about ethical excellence. These stories should fill our agility-focused lives. They should be repeated with variations to our friends, to our students, and to fellow competitors. These stories will display the particular concrete details about ethical excellence as reminders about what is good for the sport of agility. My aim is not to teach anyone *how* to be excellent. Maybe, like me, you have been striving for excellence with disappointing results. Or maybe you have actually realized excellence but still wonder what that means in a variety of different settings. If so, then together we are "partners in discovery," ideally positioned to fill in the "sketch of the good," as Aristotle puts it.

ONE

The Problem of Excellence

And that's when I start watching him, in a way I'm never able to when I'm running beside him. And yes it's true he's not a fast dog, nor is he poetry in motion or an unstoppable juggernaut or anything like that. He's a little wad of scruff with a scrap of determination, that's all (Rodi 2009, 257).

There is not just one problem of excellence in agility; there are many. But they grow out of a tangle of ideas about the concept of excellence itself, the person and her reasons for participating in the sport, the organizational structure of competitive agility, the stories we tell about our successes and failures and, of course, the very unique and complex relationship between an agility handler and her dog. In this chapter I hope to convince the reader that there are indeed problems about excellence in agility. This prepares the way to thoughtfully consider solutions to these problems as they emerge in later chapters.

The Story of Dusty

Let's begin our inquiry about excellence with a memoir by Robert Rodi (2009), *Dogged Pursuit: My Year of Competing Dusty, the World's Least Likely Agility Dog. Dogged Pursuit* is about Dusty, a novice dog and his novice handler, Rob. Rob readily admits that he has much to learn in his pursuit of "glory," as he calls it. Initially, glory means making Dusty into an agility champion by acquiring qualifying runs, ribbons, and A.K.C. titles during a year of competition. But failure lurks at almost every turn in almost every course he runs. It is both comic and, unfortunately, resonates with my own feelings of disappointment in the world of competitive agility. Even though Dusty and Rob do earn their Novice Jumpers (JWW) title, *glory* seems ridiculously out of reach.

> He follows refusal with refusal, to the point that I have to wonder what he thinks we're doing out here anyway, just having a nice stroll among all this pretty equipment?... I storm out in a kind of blind rage. This entire weekend has been an unmitigated disaster, heaping indignity upon indignity, humiliation upon humiliation [Rodi 2009, 146, 183].

There is quite a bit more to Rob's story than these despairing comments, including what *glory* comes to mean beyond the chase for points and titles. I'll come back to that later. But now take a moment to reflect on your own agility experiences, not those that were full of grace. Not those few runs or sequences that made you feel smooth, athletic, and in perfect harmony with your dog. Rather, think about your practice or competitive runs that were possibly painful episodes, those that might be described as "ragged," "incoherent," or leading to "a hot mess of a frustrated, barky dog." I remind the reader about these examples only to situate most of us in the category of amateur athletes, those whose accomplishments may well be displays of will, effort, thoughtfulness, constancy, and resilience in the practice of our sport. But also those agility enthusiasts whose actual performances are not exceptional by comparison to a small population of elite handlers and their dogs. Acknowledging this separation between the elite athletes and the commonplace athletes in agility, as well as in other sports, raises some puzzling questions about what excellence is. For example, should amateur athletes who strive for excellence and who display, for example, the virtues of determination, effort, and resilience in the face of disappointment be considered excellent? Or should attributions of excellence be reserved for the exceptional accomplishments and not the commonplace, as some writers in the philosophy of sport suggest?[1] In other words, does the *realization* of extraordinary performance matter more than the *quest* for excellence (see Kretchmar 2019)?

This question might seem excessively theoretical for most

One. The Problem of Excellence

practitioners of the sport. Why should we care about the distinction between striving for excellence and realizing it? The most intuitive and immediate answer I can provide is to tell a story about what striving looks like when it pulls apart from actually realizing excellence in agility performance. The kind of story I have in mind will locate us inside the emotional center of these two positions: striving and realizing. For example, Robert Rodi's story about his quest for "glory" is poignant. While it is specific to Rob and his dog, Dusty, it is also representative of more general conditions experienced by most serious amateur athletes, myself included. So let's read the story of Rob and Dusty in order to focus on the emotional aspects of the story, the way in which striving for excellence shapes the very nature of what it means to practice the sport of agility.

Rob's ambitions develop slowly. He begins by taking a few classes and learning how to train his first dog, Carmen, to negotiate the obstacles on an agility course. Then, as Rob puts it, "we crossed the Rubicon and went pro, traveling to agility trials around the Midwest." When Carmen is no longer physically fit enough to continue to do agility, Rob formulates a plan to realize *glory* as a "quantifiable achievement." Rob finds a rescue dog named Dusty who has been repeatedly rejected for adoption. Rob vows to rewrite Dusty's life story by pledging to train this "scrawny, scruffy, unsmiling little beast" to compete at the highest level of mastery in agility: a national championship. In one year.

Dusty's training is hit or miss. Dusty is compliant but, as Rob notices, "he never once seemed to enjoy it—never got that look of wild delirium that comes over most dogs when they're performing at their peak—but I couldn't fault him otherwise. Maybe, I thought, if we just keep at it, the joy will come" (38). After training for more than a year they are ready to compete despite the fact that Dusty does not seem to demonstrate "championship material." Rob is hoping to achieve a qualifying run or "Q." Dusty must run the obstacles under the course time and perform with a minimum number of faults (refusals, dropped bars, etc.) for the Novice entry level. So when Dusty does finally finish a run with no faults, Rob is bereft when he learns that the run was woefully over the standard course time; no Q. There are an infinite number of ways in which achieving

Canine Agility and the Meaning of Excellence

a qualifying run can go awry, and Rob has included most of these in his accounts of trialing Dusty. The descriptions are both hilarious and wretched. Here is just one example.

> We begin well: I get him set up perfectly at the starting line, and he holds his sit-stay like a real champ. When I get the nod from the timekeeper to begin, I lead him out to the first jump and call, "Over!" He behaves as if both the concept and the word are completely alien to him. He circles the jump, looks right past the bar, at one point even ducks under it—and the more I shout "Over!" the more the command seems to turn to butterflies in the air and cavort about his head without ever touching him. And thus it goes for pretty much the whole course.... Halfway through he does execute a half-hearted jump, which not only knocks down the bar but both sides of its frame as well [Rodi 2009, 53–54].

Of course, it doesn't all go wrong, all the time. When Rob and Dusty finally do finish a course with no faults, it is time to celebrate. "We've done what we've come to do. We've Q'd. I feel exultant—like there should be a ticker-tape parade in our honor, dancing girls, a presentation from the mayor, a guest slot on *Conan* or *Leno*" (86). This success is followed by another qualifying run and a first-place blue ribbon. For Rob this is confirmation that they are "on a roll" and that much closer to competing at the national championship. *Glory* is achieved at still another competition when Rob and Dusty actually qualify in a second jumper's run to earn their Novice Jumpers title.

In more reflective moments Rob reassesses what *glory* means. He admits that at one time he believed that this might mean qualifying runs, ribbons, and titles. But he later admits that what it really means is "taking my relationship with Dusty to its highest level," specifically, "harmony, sympathy, congruity—translated into movement, grace, achievement—for me and my dog." But even after more failed attempts in the ring that are embarrassing, mortifying, and infuriating, Rob is still spellbound by the chase to create a champion agility dog. He realizes that a champion is not "always the handler or the dog that scores the highest or wins the most ribbons." Nonetheless, what continues to propel Rob onward is his belief that taking Dusty to his upper limit is "just a matter of focus, firmness, consistency, and hard work."

One. The Problem of Excellence

When Rob breaks his leg he asks his partner, Jeffrey, to take Dusty to agility class and to continue to compete him in trials they have already entered. This is an unlikely partnership but one that surprisingly seems to work, much to Rob's chagrin. There is a moment when Rob can see something in his dog that eluded him until he takes up a point of view outside of the ring, watching Jeffrey run Dusty. "I'm aware as never before that as fiercely loyal as he may be, he doesn't disappear when I'm not there. In fact, outside my shadow he seems to grow larger—as does his integrity, his *honor*" (Rodi 2009, 257).

If the story of Rob and Dusty ended right here, we might understand that the idea of striving to be a champion had undergone some revision. We might believe that Rob had reevaluated the idea that "glory" in the form of ribbons and titles is the measure of excellence. But not exactly. When Rob admits that Jeffrey is well suited to the agility community and is a quick learner both in practice and in competitions, he regretfully relinquishes his own aspirations with Dusty. Jeffrey is now the one who is "obsessed with qualifying" Dusty, taking him to competitions and walking courses, chumming around with the agility community, and bringing home stories from trials. But Rob refuses to criticize; he even feels a "twinge of envy." Instead, a new idea begins to take shape, and that is to realize his dream by adopting another rescue dog, a Collie this time. By the Collie rescue description and photo, Harley "gives off a definite whiff of crazy." That's just fine by Rob. It seems he's quite comfortable with crazy.

In agility observers can testify to displays of exceptional performance. We are awed by talent and training, quickness and smooth handling, accuracy, and style. But what do we say when striving for excellence pulls apart from actually realizing excellence? This is a question that is almost impossible to ask when we restrict our observations to elite performers in agility or in other sports. When exceptional performance is not realized there are questions to be asked, puzzles to be solved, tension, and emotional dissonance. For these very reasons we can better explore competing ideas of what excellence is when striving falls short of realizing exceptional performance. For Rob, the outcome of failing to achieve exceptional performance is "embarrassment and abashment." Despite occasional success, Rob genuinely agonizes, and it is clear that some of this torment is experienced by Dusty as well. Call this the psychological disvalue that accompanies striving for excellence and falling short, over and over again. Presumably it is the humiliation and feelings of self-defeat that underlie Rob's intention to give up his competitive agility ambitions altogether.

Moral Character and Excellence

The memoir about Rob and Dusty illustrates how striving and failing to achieve excellence can act like an emotional wrecking ball. But if we read more carefully we also see an alternative storyline, one that depicts Rob's determination, persistence, and grit. On this view excellence may consist of those moral values of resilience, constancy, and the will to endure physical and psychological hardships. In the larger arena of sport Kretchmar (2019, 368) identifies these values as "intensity of meaning, purposeful caring, and ardent striving."

This alternative account of excellence does not entail the realization of exceptional performance. Instead, the criteria for excellence are located in the values that produce performance, no matter how commonplace that performance is. It doesn't necessarily follow from this alternative account that every athlete is excellent. Rather, we applaud the population of athletes whose will or intentions to succeed prevail over all else. This may include the golfer who tries time after time to score 99. It may include the tennis player who practices her serve four or five times a week in order to compete gracefully in the senior tennis league. And for sure the population of excellent athletes captured by this alternative account will include Rob and Dusty who, in spite of their calamitous trialing performances, manage to display the will and tenacity to continue to compete.

For example, the assumption that lies at the heart of Rob's striving is that if he and Dusty continue to try, try, try to be champions, then this outcome will be eventually realized. When Rob wants to rally himself back into the game after so much discouragement, he says, "I remind myself that the whole point of this agility adventure is to shake off that shroud of timorousness and restraint. To be bold,

One. The Problem of Excellence

to be heroic, to strive and achieve. I need it, Dusty needs it—it's high time we went out there and just *did* it" (Rodi 2009, 77). The idea that grips Rob is the struggle of champions. In yet another moment of dejection Rob decides not to return to the trial for the second day. It has just gone horribly badly; he barely finds the effort or the will to endure another discouraging collection of runs.

By profiling intention and will as the essential criteria we relax the standard of excellence in such a way that it can be applied to more sporting enthusiasts. Maybe even I am excellent according to this sense of excellence—a surprising consequence indeed. Some might argue that the difficulty with equating this kind of noble striving with what it means to be excellent is that we have cheapened the concept of excellence. In other words, if more athletes are excellent, then the value of their achievements is diminished (Kretchmar 2019, 373).

There is quite a bit more to be said about each of these positions: excellence as the realization of exceptional performance and excellence as will or intention. These two contrasting poles about excellence form just two possibilities that we will explore further in Chapters Two and Three. But for now consider another example of striving for excellence in the sport of agility, one that brings about a different kind of psychological disvalue for the handler as well as for the dog she loves.

Maggie's Online Trials[2]

I set her up at the start line, three feet before the first jump. *This* time we will go clean. I'll edit the front and back of the video to under 90 seconds. Then I'll upload it to the UK Agility International (U.K.I.) Facebook page for Beginner/Novice Agility 1 online course trial for week five. That's the plan and it sounds easy enough. Except we don't go clean on the first run. Maggie skirts the A-frame because I didn't cue it. Maybe I expected her to just run up the ramp? Well, she followed me instead. So I set her up at the start line again, for the second time. This run goes better at the A-frame, but she has too much speed going into the weave poles and misses her entrance.

Canine Agility and the Meaning of Excellence

The author's dog, Maggie, looking happy on the dogwalk. SAAC Trial at High Goal Farm, September 2020 (photograph by David K. Cerilli).

Again, I train the poles by sending her in correctly. And once more I line her up at the start. You can see how this is going. But in the grip of the moment, I don't get it yet. We try to run the course for a third time but she knocks a bar and then just avoids another jump, stopping to sniff. My high-drive, fun-loving, energetic Australian Shepherd has just voted with her paws. She might be saying, "I don't understand this…. I don't want to keep running this same sequence over and over and over again."

Like many of my agility friends, during the years 2020–2021 perhaps you were craving competition and searching high and low for trials to enter. But during this time most face-to-face trials were canceled. To accommodate the interests of the agility community some organizations sponsored online trialing. U.K.I. posts their online trial courses to enter and then invites members to construct the courses in their own backyards or at local facilities that allow for small numbers of people to gather by law of that state. Some of my

One. The Problem of Excellence

agility classmates wanted to try the U.K.I. trialing, so we entered the same classes and set up the course to run one day a week, filming our efforts. The general idea is a good one. And judging from the posted runs on the U.K.I. Facebook page, many handlers and their dogs all over the world are successfully running these courses and acquiring points to move up or title. So I'm genuinely glad that there is this opportunity available. U.K.I. is smart and responsive to all of us trying to keep doing competitive agility.

The rules for online trialing with U.K.I. allow for any amount of practice and any number of runs that will help you and your dog run clean on the course that you purchase by entering a class. There is a requirement to include a 10-second clip of you and your dog before and after you run. This allows the judges a chance to evaluate that your dog is in good condition. The entire video cannot be more than 90 seconds. But what does it feel like from the inside, trying to produce a clean run that counts as an acceptable video to post? I could devote this chapter section to all of the problems that arise with technology (filming, editing, uploading...). These details are sometimes challenging and rather distracting. But what I really want to think about more and share is the psychology of participating in these online trials. I don't just mean my own emotional and intellectual states, but also how I believe my dog, Maggie, is fairing under these conditions.

Identifying and practicing any challenging handling sequences is a crucial first step. I didn't realize this until my instructor reminded me that I didn't just have to run the course from start to finish just like I would do at a trial. So, after walking the course, my first runs with Maggie were short sequences that looked a little tricky. Toys and treats are included as part of my dog's first "look." And then the cameras roll. I don't bother to keep the film clip short by turning my tablet on and off. I just let it run, recording everything for a 10- to 14-minute interval. But as my earlier description reveals, an infinite number of things can go wrong. Somewhere between the second (and third, fourth, or even fifth) attempt to run the course, I've forgotten about my dog. I may have given her a rest for a while, so it's not as if she is overheated, exhausted, or physically drained. But slowly and gradually, in my mind, she has become a *tool* for generating a *product* which is the finished video capturing a clean run. I emphasize the words "tool" and "product" because they point in an entirely different way to what we imagine we are doing with our dogs when we train, or even when we participate in face-to-face trials.

Normally we think of tools as objects that are used to make something or to create an end product like a chair or a new roof on the deck. And, of course, tools can be well made, easy to use, and long-lasting as opposed to shoddily made, awkward to use, and quick to break. So we can admire and appreciate tools for their useful properties. The useful properties of tools are defined by how well they function relative to their manufactured purpose. A saw is good only if it can cut. It was made for that purpose. A straight edge is good (and useful) only if it is actually straight and can be used to measure and align. In other words, the central idea about tools as artifacts is that they are instruments, man-made objects that serve a purpose or end.

So when I characterize Maggie as a tool, even temporarily, I am saying something like "I am using you, Maggie, as an instrument to produce a 90-second video of an agility run with no faults." Do I always think of her in this way? Of course not! But the temptation is built into the task itself since it is possible to try again and again to produce a video that I can post. I believe this possibility may affect each one of us differently. What I notice about myself is that the prospect of running a course clean is seductive. It's like a drug that gets a grip on me even after I've consciously decided that I'm going to cut my losses for this week's trial. It will occur to me two days later that, in fact, I still have 24 hours to edit and to upload the video if only I have *another* chance to run the course clean.

The psychology that is difficult for me to dislodge is that I am trying to produce something. And that thing I am trying to produce in this context is not what we normally think we are doing when we train (or play) agility with our dogs. For example, a training session where Maggie drops a bar is an opportunity for reflection. Was it just a slip on the grass or was it something I can fix? With my instructor's help I might think about my handling, my dog's approach, her speed, or what we might need to do in order to facilitate a change in the quality of her jumping. But when I am recording a run to post for an online trial, a dropped bar means "Darn! We didn't do it. Now we

One. The Problem of Excellence

have to start from the beginning of the course again." So that's the sense in which I've forgotten about Maggie herself. Temporarily, my desire for a product is the measure of success. In other words, I'm using my beautiful, intelligent, absurdly enthusiastic agility partner like a well-crafted saw that functions efficiently to cut wood.

I've explained my online trial experience from the inside, what it feels like for me. But what about Maggie? If she could speak, what would she say about these trials? It's pretty obvious by paying attention to her behavior. And I know her. Maggie likes to run full-tilt. Her first runs in class and also at trials are fast and furious. This is not ideal. We make mistakes because I'm just learning how to handle her from a distance so that I can stay ahead of her on the course, just barely. But what I admire about these mad dashes is how Maggie is so clearly invested in following me and looking to the next obstacle. "Show me! Where, *where* do I go next? Quick! Wait, I see it. There's a [jump, tunnel, teeter]; I'll go there!" In other words, she's all in. And, weirdly, she wasn't always like this. In her first year of agility, Maggie was mostly compliant and willing although a little distracted. But now she is "drive-y." I only mention this quality because I value it more than anything else. It makes me ridiculously happy to see her attack an agility course at full throttle. And perhaps it is confirmation that she loves her job and will happily do this sport with me.

Because of all that I know about Maggie, I finally take notice in my online trialing efforts when she refuses the first jump and sniffs the ground instead. And I finally take notice when she veers away from a jump that is right on her path. What have I produced now? My feeling of regret tells me everything. I do feel disappointed about not creating a video of a clean run. But this is not the source of my increasing remorse. It is that my once happy, fast, and enthusiastic agility partner is no longer willing. I have squandered that very quality that I love about her. Can she forgive me? Can I make it up to her? I know this doesn't make a lot of sense. But I vow to pay more attention to my dog in the immediate future by only training short sequences with *lots* of rewards. This week I will not be entering an online trial.

What deserves more reflection is how the online trialing experience is the same and/or different from face-to-face trialing. Here are my "novice" thoughts. As we all know, at a face-to-face trial you get one shot. Every course you enter and run can go awry for so many reasons that have nothing to do with how well your dog is trained, or even how well you handle a sequence. An accidental dropped bar, a distracting bark, or uneven lighting on the course can all contribute to missing a clean, qualifying run. This is also true about online trialing. The difference, I believe, is how we respond to these attempts. At a face-to-face trial I may be disappointed but I know in advance that there are no "do-overs." We had a fair opportunity and one that revealed some things I can work on at home to improve my own handling ability and the skills of my dog. But running a trial course at home is an entirely different set of circumstances. For a perfectionist like myself, the temptation to do it perfectly is too hard to resist. I don't even think it is points I'm chasing even though a clean run will result in that outcome. To me what is seriously seductive about the online trial experience is that it is *possible* to rewind the clock to do the run flawlessly. I suspect this admission tells you way too much about my own obsessiveness. But some of you may share this quality of character. If so, remember to fight the very seductive temptation to repeat, repeat, and repeat. In other words, remember your dog. Maggie doesn't much care about whether we record a clean run. But she does care about pleasing me. To earn her respect and love I'm trying to be a better *trainer*. This may mean forgoing the online trialing until I self-impose some very strict limits about how we practice and run an online trial course.

Some Questions About Exceptional Performance

Looking back now on those multiple failed attempts to post a video of a clean run still almost brings me to tears. Why couldn't I see in the moment how my intense aspirations interfered with the most precious part of the activity itself, my dog, Maggie? Of course, the despair that I feel about this is specific to me. But like the story of Rob and Dusty, my story represents more general features that apply to other handlers and their dogs, situated in similar situations. One such feature is the deleterious effect of striving for excellence as exceptional performance and failing to achieve it. For Rob and Dusty the exceptional performance they aspired to achieve was becoming a champion by earning qualifying runs, ribbons, and titles. For me, moving up to the next level in U.K.I. was not primarily what I cared about. Rather, it was the perfection of a particular run as documented by video. Of course in this case what counts as "perfection" is to produce a qualifying run: no faults and under the standard course time allowed. But instead of conceding that we did not run the course clean after two or three attempts, the online trialing environment lured me back again and again, teasing me to be perfect. In both of these stories there is discernable emotional distress experienced by both handler and dog. I earlier called this the psychological disvalue of striving and failing to achieve exceptional performance. But that is not my only point of emphasis.

Each of these stories, in slightly different ways, raises questions about the nature of exceptional performance. When striving radically pulls apart from realizing or achieving, it is only natural to ask who is setting the bar and why it is set exactly there. Novak (1976, 5) characterizes performance exceptionalism as "the momentary attainment of perfect form ... [where] the curtains of ordinary life part, and perfection flashes for an instant before the eye." I am struck by Novak's claim that perfection is fleeting and short-lived. In fact, this account of exceptional performance allows that excellence might be achieved irrespective of winning. Indeed, there is no obvious reason why achieving exceptional performance in agility should be necessarily associated with what we are calling the qualifying run. So who sets this particular standard of excellence? And why do so many agility practitioners embrace this standard so enthusiastically? Some theories about excellence deserve closer scrutiny. In Chapter Two I focus on the very popular view that excellence just is exceptional performance.

Why Agility?

If we ask why agility enthusiasts undertake the sport and why they passionately pursue this activity, only a few will say that they are

Canine Agility and the Meaning of Excellence

hoping for perfection when running a course or hoping to achieve a championship title in competition.[3] Instead the activity of agility is often described as a game that we play with our dogs. JoLee Yeddo is a Canine Performance Events (C.P.E.) judge who also trains and competes in C.P.E. competitive trials. I asked JoLee what it means to "play" the game of agility, as a trainer and as a competitor.

> Yeah. It's definitely a game. Everything should be fun. Things for us, as people, are more rewarding if they're fun. Undertaking a job means you have to do it and you're going to do it well. But it may not be fun. I don't particularly love cleaning garbage cans at the end of a trial. It's a job that has to get done, so I will do it. And I will smile while I'm doing it because it's a job. I've had jobs as a teacher where it's like, okay, it's not my favorite thing right now but I'm going to make the best of it. So when dogs and handlers play together in a game there's a big reward at the end; it's a fun, happy thing. We remember laughing more from these fun experiences and enjoying them. If we laugh a lot, we remember those things.... When [the dog] is at the end of the run and their whole body is wriggling or they're jumping, they're hopping, and they're just celebrating what they just accomplished with you, it's like they are saying, "We just did this thing and it was great!" And that's why when I get to the end of the run, whether or not we did it right, I want them to celebrate that we did something together. That was really cool. There's a celebration. If it's a game then it's not just work.

There is much more to be said about what it means to *play* agility. But one challenge for this characterization of agility is where to locate excellence. Some ways of playing just produce simple pleasures. For example, a baby who plays in her bathwater, splashing the water here and there, is just having a delightful experience. And some games are not rule-bound. Throwing a ball up in the air to catch (or not) or throwing a Frisbee to a dog does not necessarily involve standards of correctness, rules, or acquired skills. So if agility is a game we play with our dogs, then what exactly do we mean by playing? And what kind of game is it? In Chapter Three I explore some possible answers to these questions. This will tell us whether or not it makes sense to say that standards of excellence apply to agility as play.

One. The Problem of Excellence

Agility as Hobby

When the Bad Dog Agility podcast hosts asked listeners to explain why they love agility, they received a variety of answers, as we might expect.[4] Naturally some people love the thrill of competition and the challenge of training. The hosts emphasized that because many practitioners of agility come from a sports background, they are drawn to the acquisition of skills and the testing of proficiency in the competitive setting. But far more commonly respondents said that they valued being connected with their dogs. They wanted to build a relationship with their canine athletes in order to witness and to celebrate their capabilities, athleticism, and intelligence. This population of enthusiasts wanted to understand how their dogs learned. So it was the process of practice and training that they prized rather than the competitive trialing per se. In other words, this informal survey revealed that for most people agility is not a professional pursuit but a hobby. "It's just fun" is a suitable answer to the question "Why do you love agility?" The hobbyist is the central player in Chapter Four. Consider Wayne Booth (1999) who took up the cello late in life. He claims that even though amateurs are seeking perfection, the purpose of the hobbyist's pursuit (playing the cello, practicing agility) is puzzling since success is impossibly out of reach. "Why go on taking lessons and practicing daily when every playing session demonstrates that you will *always* play worse than every cellist, even the worst, in the youth orchestra you heard last week" (Booth 1999, 6)?

If agility is merely a hobby, then it is not clearly and obviously an activity that occupies the sphere of competitive sport. What excellence means in competitive sports is fairly straightforward. This involves ranking competitors, thereby measuring their success. The aim is to win. But LaVaque-Manty (2009, 143) distinguishes this context from what she calls "recreational sports." In most cases recreational athletes don't aim to win. Recreational athletes "don't aim at excellence at all." Rather they participate "for health, to raise funds for a charity, to have fun with friends—in short, for recreation."

Amateur, n. A public nuisance who mistakes taste for skill, and confounds his ambition with his ability [Bierce, n.d.].

Okay, this definition of an amateur is a bit uncharitable. But the challenge in Chapter Four is still to show how excellence may find its natural home in activities described as hobbies undertaken by amateur agility enthusiasts.

Agility Organizations

Does the concept of excellence fluctuate across handlers, dogs, and circumstances? If so, then who sets the standards of excellence? Perhaps each of us gets to determine for ourselves whether or not a particular moment of agility is excellent. As tempting as this view sounds, it cannot be right. Agility is situated in an institutional context that includes many different agility organizations: the American Kennel Club (A.K.C.), the Australian Shepherd Club of America (A.S.C.A.), Canine Performance Events (C.P.E.), and so on. Each organization specifically articulates rules for competitive agility trialing. If we use these organizations as a guide, the standards of excellence are settled, at least for competitors. The basic unit of value across all agility organizations is the qualifying run. The institutions that oversee competitive trialing use this measure of excellence to determine who accrues points, titles, and championships. Invariably we observe our own trialing experiences through this same lens. Chapter Five introduces an alternative point of view about what should count as excellence. Perhaps agility practitioners should associate excellence with what I am calling the internal rewards and core relational values of the activity.

Training Excellence

The problem of training excellence is not about how to train a dog to display exceptional performance. Chapter Six explores how training can facilitate what I believe are the necessary ingredients of excellence: the relational values of respect, trust, and communication. So the challenge of this chapter is to find points of intersection between a certain description of training and those particular concepts that form the core of excellence in agility. This is no small task because there are competing accounts of what it means to train a dog. Similarly, there is unclarity about what it means to realize mutual respect, mutual trust, and mutual communication between humans and nonhumans. For example, some philosophical ideas about respect are abstractions. They credit animals, including dogs, with a rich mental life that entails beliefs, desires, and emotions. This in turn justifies attributing autonomy and agency to an animal. The abbreviated argument for animal rights, including the right to respectful treatment, depends on crediting nonhuman animals with autonomy and a kind of agency. But the real-world relationships between humans and dogs is absent from this typical philosophical discussion of rights and respect. So what I want to know is what respect, trust, and communication look like on the ground, so to speak, when training a dog. We have to talk to trainers themselves to find out.

Telling Stories

In the chapters that follow I make use of stories about agility. Some of these are true, some are based in truth, and some are fiction. So it is fair to ask what role stories play in the analysis of excellence in agility. The answer is that the idea of excellence is shaped by the stories we tell about our sport. The challenge is to tell a story in such a way that it captures the point of view of the handler, the point of view of the dog, and the complex and exquisite relationship that binds them both together.

Introducing Sue Hall

Sue Hall has been a constant presence in my agility class that meets on Tuesdays at 10:00 a.m. at Aussie Acres Agility with instructor Robin Magee. I think we have been seeing each other at exactly this time for the last five or six years. We have run our dogs together in hot, hot weather, in the pouring rain and, believe it or not, in the

Canine Agility and the Meaning of Excellence

Sue Hall is staying connected with her dog, Esther. Agility lesson with Robin Magee at Aussie Acres Agility, October 2023 (photograph by Sue Lezon).

snow. Two years ago we actually shoveled snow off the path between obstacles in order to stay outside for just one more week! Sue and her little Irish terrier, Esther, keep us all laughing. They are both full of energy and exuberance, running the sequences and courses fast and furious, and with joy. Initially, I believed that Sue was froth on the wave. Her laughing and joking made me think that she wasn't all that serious about the work and the sport. Boy, was I ever wrong. She may not be somber about what she and Esther do together in the ring, but she is indeed dedicated to improving her own handling skills as well as Esther's training. Sue was my first choice to interview because she is devoted and earnest about agility, but she does no competitive trialing. This gives her a unique perspective about what it means to be excellent.

How did you start doing agility?

Well, I swam at the Y.M.C.A. for about 30 years, and I taught there also. That's where I met Karen, who told me about agility class

One. The Problem of Excellence

at Aussie Acres. My last dog before Esther was a Frisbee dog, and Karen said, "Oh you would like agility because it's a lot of jumping."

I knew that the breed [Irish terrier] is not a great listener and they're very distractible, but I said, "I'm going to try agility. That's a challenge." I picked a dog that they say isn't ideal for a beginner owner, and I've done pretty well in some areas with her and not so well in other areas.

Hey, I do marathons. Yeah. I'm not fast, but I got old and I could run, so I qualified in Boston. I played tennis for a while. I mean, I just like activity: hiking, biking, and triathlons. So I knew if agility was an athletic endeavor that I would like it. Plus, I like being outside.

What is the most satisfying thing about doing agility? What do you love about it?

When we have a good run in class. At times I've come back and asked, "Why am I doing this?" I can't get anything to work. So I've had bad days.

But the satisfying part is when we're connected. She doesn't spin, she gets almost every sequence right. It's rare but sometimes she's really on. Some days it's just so marvelous. Just like for any athletic pursuit, it's when you're clicking and moving, it's just fun. It's just so cool when I say "in" and she goes inside of a jump, or when she goes around to wrap a jump. She looks pretty cool sometimes when she's really on.

What would you say is the most frustrating aspect about doing agility?

Well, I've been working on a couple of skills. I want her to exit the tunnel and go around the back side of a jump about 10–12 feet away. So I say "around" to do the backside of the jump from a distance. She did it eventually, but she had to spin.

Even though you don't enter competitive agility trials, are you competitive in practice?

I played tennis with people just for fun, but I would make sure I won. When I play in a game I always want to win the game. But in running events or swimming events, it's about your time and qualifying. So in agility I just want to solve problems and get a good run. I like trying to accomplish something hard.

Canine Agility and the Meaning of Excellence

Does excellence mean not making any mistakes?
    I try to figure out what the right pattern is by walking the line. And I try to figure out what's going to be the hardest thing for us to do as a team. Now I can usually guess where it's going to be fast. And if she's on, then the question is "How am I going to get to that next jump?" So even on a course that's hard, if we do make a mistake but I get the hardest part right, then it feels good. I think I show exuberance sometimes when we've had a good run; I might jump around and say "awesome." Excellence is not my word, I guess.

Do you think that the meaning of excellence should be reserved for handlers and dogs who compete and win?
    Well, that's the whole thing. Suppose you're a great pianist. Do you have to perform? I don't know. You could be an excellent piano player and never play for anyone but yourself. You definitely could be excellent in music but no one would know it but you and your teacher. It's different with sports. They're all about competing, aren't they?

Do you think that if a person is not successful at agility that you should just keep trying? Is there value in just struggling to be excellent?
    Yeah, just do what you're better at and keep going in that direction. I think there's value in just plugging away and doing it. Because if you just give up on everything it might be because you haven't figured it out yet. By the same token, if you're too good at something it's more pressure. If you're not good, it's less pressure. Right? Some people might think it's more rewarding if you're less talented or less gifted in training dogs and you still manage to do it.

Summary

    The problem of excellence in agility takes various forms. The two stories I have shared in this chapter have explanatory value for the inquiry ahead. It might seem that I have merely documented failure and how acutely that feels from the inside point of view. Of course, there is that. But I prefer that readers become alert to how we may tease apart two different senses of excellence: excellence as the

One. *The Problem of Excellence*

Sue Hall's dog, Esther, shows some style through the tire jump. Agility lesson with Robin Magee at Aussie Acres Agility, October 2023 (photograph by Sue Lezon).

realization of exceptional performance and excellence as intention or will. In the philosophy of sport there is, in fact, historical precedent for each of these views. But the theoretical literature will not reveal as vividly how this distinction is embodied and personified by practitioners of our sport in particular. Rather than lament the psychological disvalue of failing to realize excellence, we should focus instead on trying to clarify what exceptional performance is and how it is measured.

If agility is a game that we play with our dogs, then what counts as excellent play? Playing a game does not automatically imply that there exist standards of excellence, skill, or prescriptive rules. Alternatively, if agility is characterized as a hobby undertaken by amateurs, then we must scrutinize more carefully what it means to engage in a hobby. For example, do hobbyists merely "dabble" in an activity? If so, then another problem about excellence is that it may be a misplaced aspiration for amateurs.

Do agility organizations such as the A.K.C. or C.P.E. encourage a culture where excellence is understood to be the acquisition of points, titles, and championships? If so, then one problem about excellence is to imagine how the core values of excellence may survive in spite of this competitive context. In this case the demand is to articulate an alternative concept, one that can reckon with a culture of competition that values the external rewards of our sport.

A theory about excellence in agility should be broad and deep. It should be broad in the sense that it includes not just performative moments of "awe" but also the relationship between dog and handler-as-trainer. It should be deep in the sense that we preserve the core values of excellence: respect, trust, and communication between handlers and their dogs. The practical problem is to discover how training can facilitate this ethical concept of excellence.

Finally, there is a challenge lurking at the end of this book. The challenge is how to tell a story about excellence that captures what is good for the practice of agility, a *narrative* quest for excellence. This challenge is for those who are most invested in pursuing excellence in agility. That's all of us who love the sport.

Two

Exceptional Performance

> *The "achievement model of sport" ... takes its primary values from the world of work—worthy problems, the promise of progress, the need for preparation, the virtues of effort and dedication, the exercise of skill* (Kretchmar 2015, 87).

Recall from Chapter One that we considered two main positions about excellence. One is that excellence entails the realization of exceptional performance and another is that excellence privileges the moral values of striving rather than high-level achievement. Here we are focusing exclusively on the idea that excellence is explained by exceptional performance. The two stories we explored in the last chapter revealed the psychological disvalue of striving and failing to achieve exceptional performance. But what is exceptional performance anyway? Is it a qualifying run performed at a competitive trial? Is it a flawless practice run in agility class? Is it a display of skill by handler and dog in one perfect moment? I will argue that excellence is not any of these things. This is because I believe that excellence is not measured by the *realization* of exceptional performance in general. Since this is somewhat counter-intuitive to what most people believe, I will take some time to explain why I think the idea of exceptional performance does not capture what we should say about excellence in agility.

To begin this part of the inquiry, consider how some standards of excellence are described at the organizational level. For example, the American Kennel Club (A.K.C.) recognizes a "lifetime of excellence" for achieving the title *Agility Grand Champion* (AGCH). In order to achieve this kind of excellence a dog and handler must have collected the following number of qualifying scores:

- Master Standard and Master Jumpers with Weaves (JWW)—100 qualifying scores from each class;
- Master FAST—75 qualifying scores;
- Time 2 Beat—75 qualifying scores;
- Premier Standard and Premier JWW—50 qualifying scores from each class.

That's a lot of Qs! No wonder they are calling this a *"lifetime of excellence."* Clearly only a few exceptional teams have achieved excellence in this sense. But as it turns out there is no inherent necessary relation between the concept of excellence per se and a certain number of qualifying scores. In other words, measuring a lifetime of excellence in agility is a convention created by the A.K.C. Alternatively, the creators of the award could have specified that only *25 qualifying scores* are needed in each class of Premier Standard and Premier JWW instead of 50. It probably would not matter to the candidates for the Lifetime Excellence Award, although it would generate a few less dollars in entry fees for the A.K.C. Another way of illustrating the contingency of equating excellence and qualifying scores is to look across different organizational standards for earning a qualifying score.

What Is a Qualifying Run?

Take three imaginary runs with Maggie and me. We will perform each run exactly the same with some specific kinds and numbers of faults, but visualize also that each run will be performed in a competitive trial sanctioned by different organizations: A.K.C., A.S.C.A., and C.P.E. The Excellent/Master JWW course below was designed by Zach Gulaboff Davis for an A.K.C. trial sponsored by the Burlington Obedience Training Club held in Shelburne, Vermont, on July 31, 2022. Study the map as I did before running this course. Imagine the following.

Maggie runs clean and fast up to jump #11. When I send her out and over to that jump, I pull off too quickly and she drops the bar. As we approach jump #15, I rear-cross to get her on my right side for the tunnel entrance, but I cut behind her too soon. Rather

Two. Exceptional Performance

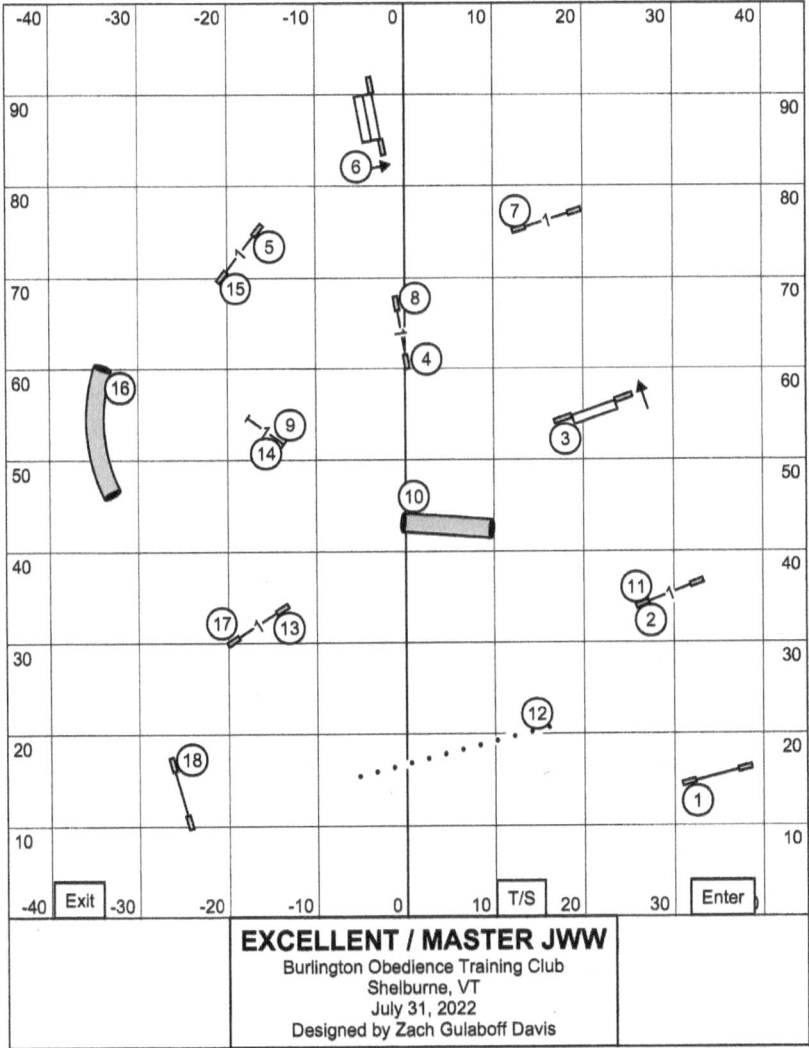

A.K.C. Excellent/Masters Jumpers with Weaves Course Map. Burlington Obedience Training Club, Shelburne, Vermont, July 31, 2022 (course design by Zach Gulaboff Davis).

than surging ahead, she runs past this jump. I call her back to me and send her again so that she jumps #15 going the right direction.

Canine Agility and the Meaning of Excellence

Our finish is smooth and fast. We come in under the standard course time.

Even though the course map is an A.K.C. Excellent/Master Jumpers with Weaves (JWW) course, we can imagine that we also run the very same course in A.S.C.A. Elite Jumpers (no weaves) and in C.P.E. Level 5 Jumpers (no weaves). What are the criteria for earning a qualifying run in each organization when the number and kinds of faults stay constant? Most of you already know the answer to this if you do competitive agility under the umbrella of more than one organization. In my imaginary scenario we incurred one dropped bar and one "refusal" when Maggie ran past the plane of jump #15. If we are running this course in an A.K.C. trial at the Excellent/Master level, this is a non-qualifying run or NQ. There are two faults recorded for the run: dropped bar and refusal. Either of these faults will be sufficient to merit an NQ. In A.S.C.A. there are no refusals. This means that when Maggie runs past the plane of jump #15, providing that she comes back around to jump it in the right direction, she will not be faulted. But the dropped bar at jump #11 is a fault. Consequently, in an A.S.C.A. trial at the Jumpers Elite level, the run will be recorded as an NQ. What about C.P.E.? C.P.E. does not fault for refusals. And C.P.E. allows for the fault of one bar down in Jumpers classes in Levels 4 and 5. So if we ran this exact same course with the exact same performance in a C.P.E. event, we would earn a Q. See the chart below for a visual representation of this outcome.

Faults	A.K.C.	A.S.C.A.	C.P.E.
One Refusal	NQ	Q	Q
One Dropped Bar	NQ	NQ	Q

I suppose it is not surprising that different agility organizations, over time, develop different criteria for what counts as a qualifying score. This variability also reaches into the kinds of courses competitors face. For example, the international agility organization, U.K.I., famously constructs courses that require much more challenging handling, using backsides of jumps even in Beginner/Novice classes. But what should give us pause is how different standards for qualifying overlay the concept of excellence. If excellence is measured

Two. Exceptional Performance

by exceptional performance, and exceptional performance is measured by a qualifying score, then the concept of excellence in agility is absurdly variable merely by virtue of the conventions of particular agility organizations. Is there a preferred criterion that might justify a default standard for a qualifying run? We might look to the mission statements of these organizations to see whether or not there is some rationale for adopting one rather than another qualifying score standard. Readers may read on their own these respective mission statements for the A.K.C.,[1] A.S.C.A.,[2] and C.P.E.[3] It seems to me that none of these include a fine-grained rationale for adopting one particular qualifying score standard. So these institutional declarations don't help to justify why qualifying in A.K.C. is measured differently from qualifying in A.S.C.A. or in C.P.E.

It is time to ask a different kind of question about excellence. One possibility that we should now consider is whether or not exceptional performance in agility *should* reduce to earning a qualifying run, no matter how easy or difficult it is to merit that qualifying score. In other words, maybe there are some qualifying runs that don't exhibit exceptional performance (or excellence). And maybe there are some non-qualifying runs that are, in fact, displays of exceptional performance (or excellence). If this is possible, then the qualifying run is not a reliable measure of excellence.

This tentative conclusion has a theoretical pedigree articulated by Nicholas Dixon (2002, 220) in an article titled "On Winning and Athletic Superiority." Here Dixon invites the reader to consider the following question: "Which team is better in a competitive sporting contest? The winner or the team or player that is superior?" The cases that interest Dixon are those where the competitive results may fail to accurately measure athletic superiority or excellence. These situations include (1) cases of refereeing errors, (2) cases where a team or player cheats or breaks the rules, (3) cases of gamesmanship, e.g., trash talking the other team, (4) cases of bad luck, and (5) cases of inferior performance by superior athletes (or vice versa). Let's apply these general situations to the practice of agility. For our purposes we will use a qualifying run to mean the same thing as what Dixon calls "winning." Only some of situations described in cases 1–5 will mark an illustrative point.

Canine Agility and the Meaning of Excellence

Case 1: In competitive agility it is certainly possible for the judge to make a mistake in calling a fault in a run. Sometimes the judge fails to see everything that happens when a fast dog barrels around 20 obstacles. Imagine that the judge fails to see that a dog missed touching the yellow on the bottom of the A-frame. This is, of course, a fault, resulting in a non-qualifying score. But if the judge does not call the fault, then perhaps the team officially receives a qualifying score and maybe they even officially won the class. Nevertheless, what we ought to say in this case is that the qualifying score does not reflect superior performance or excellence. Dixon would say that even though the team "won," they are not superior. One might argue that because the referee's (or judge's) word is final, then the decision is "just." Well, maybe. But merely because a judge has the power to call a run "qualifying" doesn't mean that he or she is infallible (Dixon, 2002, 221). The implication is that an agility team that won a class by virtue of a judging mistake does not necessarily display exceptional performance or excellence.

I will skip situations 2 and 3 because cases of cheating by breaking the rules or cases of gamesmanship are unlikely to be on display in competitive agility settings. Instead I turn to situation 4: bad luck. Certainly we can imagine what most of us would ordinarily call an exceptional performance undone by a stroke of bad luck. This may include the following: an outside trial is windy, blowing debris in and around the ring and distracting the handler and dog; an aggressive dog barks outside of the ring just as a competitor's dog enters the weave poles; a mere slip of a dog's front leg on wet grass knocks a bar down in a morning run while afternoon runs take place on dry grass. Dixon (2002, 226) says about team sports that these strokes of bad luck may mean that the dominant or superior team may still lose the competition. The same can be said about competitive agility. We see what would have been an exceptional performance undone by a momentary distraction, a slip on wet grass, or interference from outside the ring. It is still reasonable to say that in these cases exceptional performance would have been realized if not for bad luck. In other words, the losing team, or the non-qualifying team, may, in fact, be the excellent team.

Finally, consider case 5. On a particular day, an inferior

Two. Exceptional Performance

performance is displayed by a superior athlete. The reverse is also possible. The assessment that an athlete is superior may be that *typically* over time that athlete exhibits exceptional performance. In team sports this situation could be recorded as the number of wins in a league for the entire season. If in the playoffs that team is beaten, then we might say, arguably, that the inferior performance in the playoff game did not reflect the superiority of the losing team. Dixon suggests that this is a failing of the playoff system in team sports when too much emphasis is placed on one game at the end of the season. We might say something comparable about A.S.C.A. Nationals. Over the course of one year agility teams aspire to accumulate enough qualifying scores to be eligible for A.S.C.A. finals at the end of the year. But just having the highest number of points overall will not guarantee that you will win or even place in the finals held during a particular week. Anything can go wrong in those finals classes. So one consequence may be that the highest ranking dog may not even make the top 10 finalists. If exhibiting poise under pressure is a highly valued attribute of competition, then perhaps this system is the right measure of superior performance. But at least it is possible to ask the question "Does winning at A.S.C.A. Nationals Finals measure excellence?" Consider this comment by Dixon (2002, 233):

> [My] discussion of inferior performances by superior athletes (section 5) does not indicate any unfairness in the results of sporting contests. After all, the team that plays better on the day against superior opponents *deserves* to win. What my arguments in that section do show is that even a just result is sometimes not an accurate indicator of the relative athletic excellence of the teams. The only sense in which such a result is unjust is reflected in the statement that the losing team did not do justice to itself.

Dixon concludes that the rationale for his inquiry about the distinction between winning and athletic superiority is for readers to realize "that winning is not the be all and end all of athletic excellence." For our purposes Dixon's discussion about how winning pulls apart from excellence is useful for evaluating the idea that the qualifying score is a measure of excellence in agility. If winning (or qualifying) does not reliably or accurately reflect excellence, then what does?

Canine Agility and the Meaning of Excellence

Tiny, Beautiful Moments

One consequence of adopting exceptional performance as the criterion for excellence is that it restricts the class of excellent athletes to elite performers only. Striving for excellence with determination and effort is not sufficient, although it may well accompany high-level accomplishment. Kretchmar (2015, 87) calls this the "achievement model of sport," where athletes pursue "excellence in the form of extraordinary achievement or success, and earning and deserving the honor or respect that goes with it."

"Extraordinary achievement or success" is a general description of excellence, but it has the potential to individuate cases of excellence in a more fine-grained way than is measured by earning a qualifying score in agility. Let's call these "tiny, beautiful moments" (Strayed, 2012). Recall Novak's (1969, 5) description of performance exceptionalism (from Chapter One).

> Athletic achievement ... is the momentary attainment of perfect form—as though there were, hidden away from mortal eyes, a perfect way to execute a play and suddenly a player or a team has found it and sneaked a demonstration down to earth. A great play is a revelation. The curtains of ordinary life part, and perfection flashes for an instant before the eye.

So if we are looking for excellence in agility beyond the qualifying score, then we might focus instead on the tiny, beautiful moments where "perfection flashes for an instant before the eye." And what are we looking for exactly? Most of us who train agility dogs, practice daily drills or exercises, or who compete in agility will have no trouble generating a list of valued skills that can be mastered and displayed by both handler and dog. Let's identify a few of these skills specific to agility although we may not capture all of them.

To begin, we can speak generally about reciprocity between handler and dog (Lund 2014, 102). This involves companionship as well as judgment, communication, and responsibility that will be on display in moments of excellence. What does this look like when it is realized in the practice of agility? Imagine a long, 20-foot send to a tunnel. When I say "tunnel" Maggie drives ahead of me even though we are two jumps away from the entrance. She is honoring my verbal

Two. Exceptional Performance

command. But now suppose that the correct tunnel entrance is the near side, not the side she is immediately facing on the approach, a typical challenge in a more advanced course. Now things are different. I need to let her know with my opposite arm raised to pull her toward me, and maybe a verbal "close," just in time to allow her to readjust her line. If it works then we are each responsible for the successful sequence. I am responsible for letting her know early where we are going, and Maggie is responsible for following my body and voice. I know that she is trying so hard to figure out what I want, but if I am a fraction of a second too late, it makes all the difference. This might count as an instance of communication and teamwork demonstrated by each of us "running with precision and gusto" (Lund 2014, 108).

Of course, not everything is always so perfect. I don't always trust my dog. This is a kind of failure that I am trying hard to correct. The way it sometimes manifests is to send Maggie to a jump and then pause to see if she actually jumps. This is her job, of course. It is her responsibility. But I often wait and watch to see if she will *actually* jump. Many aficionados of agility know that this is a recipe for disaster with a fast dog because it puts the handler behind for the next sequence. In a fraction of a second my run goes to ruin. All of a sudden Maggie is ahead of me and wonders, "What's next?" She genuinely doesn't know because I waited too long at the last jump. And now she is distraught. Maggie is a dog who does not suffer fools. If I make a mistake at my end, she will articulate her frustration by jumping up, grabbing my shirt or arm with her teeth, and sometimes even breaking the skin through several layers of clothing. This is, most definitely, not a display of excellence. I think of it as a momentary failure of trust. Weirdly, in the very same run this event may occur immediately following a magnificent off-side tunnel send. So we have on display how moments of excellence in a competition or practice run may be bookended by less than exceptional teamwork and communication. Exceptional performance is sometimes only a momentary display of skill. The general characteristics of excellence, however, involve cooperation, teamwork, watching each other, trusting, and confidence to produce a competitive run that is accurate and fast (Lund 2014, 109).

Skills

If you spend any time on the sidelines of an agility trial as a spectator or as an exhibitor, you get to see a lot of runs. Multiply this by the number of trials entered during a particular month and you will understand how variable performance looks from the outside point of view. This point of view is instructive because you can witness highly skilled dogs with highly skilled handlers and rather poor or sloppy handlers with skilled dogs that have learned to compensate or "read" their handler's imperfect cues as well as experienced handlers who are attempting to run a young dog with emergent skills or a difficult dog that is in re-training. Agility skills emerge somewhat incrementally for handler and dog in practice and training. But these are not merely physical skills since the mental aspect of skillfulness also may include nerve or courage or patience (Campos 2014, 370). Most agility enthusiasts have accumulated a collection of articles, books, podcasts, seminars, workshops, and online courses in order to cultivate the skills that are highly valued in practice or in competition.[4] I can't possibly review them all. But how do these skills *generally* manifest in our evaluations of exceptional performance?

We testify to exceptional performance when an agility dog has successfully interpreted a cue for a difficult sequence. She (the dog) might display discrimination about how to approach the weave poles, or how to push to the backside of a jump, or when to judge that the line of obstacles is a "go" line by surging ahead of her handler. Not only does the dog have to learn the criteria for the proper performance of each kind of obstacle, she must also respond to her handler's cues immediately after each obstacle, turning and changing direction when the next sequence is indicated. In other words, the package of skills we credit to agility dogs includes handler focus as well as obstacle focus and the ability to make discriminations between these in a fraction of a second.

We expect the handler to have some skills also. She must learn to watch her dog above all else. I can't tell you how many times I have turned my head just to watch Maggie sail over an off-course jump or even knock down a bar simply because I didn't have my eyes on her and allowed us to become disconnected. Additionally, my

Two. Exceptional Performance

trainer is always telling her students to look at the dog's path. What does the dog see? Where will she land after a jump? And what will my dog, in particular, do at this point in the run? Handlers are also urged to think about how we can help our dogs early in order to prepare for the next obstacle and sequence. Skills are acquired gradually, of course, with lots of practice. But when handling is performed smoothly and efficiently on one occasion, and the dog reads the handling with precision and speed on that same occasion, then we witness moments of exceptional performance or excellence.

When Do We Cheer, and for Whom?

To this point I have been describing some ideal conditions of exceptional performance. As I suggested, this is not *merely* reducible to earning a qualifying score in a competitive run. Instead excellence may be situated in tiny, beautiful moments when the skills of handler and dog are on fleeting display, like flashes of brilliance. But now I will challenge even this more modest characterization of excellence. In the culture of competitive agility trials, the spectators, who are mostly competitors, occasionally cheer their approval for certain dogs or certain handlers when they complete a course or even part of a course. I have never thought much about this very common but unspoken practice until now. Of course, cheering for the competition suggests that those of us who participate in the sport of agility are largely friendly and encouraging toward other entrants. But I also believe that the particular contexts for cheering—when we cheer, and for whom—reveals a more complex evaluation of excellence than we have described up to now.

Let me describe one example from my own collection of imperfect competitive experiences. Maggie began to break her start-line after about two years of competitive trialing. Make no mistake. I let her break the start once, and then it was hard to get it back. So, with some encouragement from my instructor, I sacrificed a few competitive runs to train her at the start. In other words, I declared to the judge that I was "training" and brought Maggie into the ring with a toy in hand. I set her up behind the first jump, told her to "stay,"

Canine Agility and the Meaning of Excellence

and then walked out beyond the second jump and waited. Of course, she broke her start as I predicted; she left before I released her with "okay." So I brought her back to the start line, set her up again, and walked out to the second jump just as before. This time she waited. When I released her, she jumped, she tugged with the toy as a reward, and then I tugged with her all the way back to the exit gate. Surprisingly, my fellow competitors cheered. Why? It wasn't skillful handling involving complicated turns or cues, nor did Maggie expertly negotiate an intricate sequence of obstacles. So this incident fails to conform to what we previously described as exceptional performance. Still there was something pristine about what Maggie and I did in the ring for 45 seconds that elicited applause. We had a training moment. Everyone ringside knew that we were struggling. They knew what I needed to do, and they knew what Maggie needed to learn about start lines. So the applause acknowledged the realization of success that was specific to a struggling novice team at this particular point in their competitive trialing. The applause signaled a moment of perfection for us in particular.

Now that I am alert to the culture of cheering at agility trials, I've observed a variety of other occasions for doing so. The audience cheers when a differently-abled handler maneuvers her dog through a course in a wheelchair, no matter how many faults accrue. The audience cheers when a shy dog is coaxed around the course, even if that dog is slow and is afraid to jump many of the obstacles on the course. The audience cheers even when a young dog runs wildly around the ring, ignoring his handler, if that dog goes through one tunnel before exiting. And the audience cheers when a young person or "junior" handler guides a dog through a course, no matter how imperfect the handling is or how the dog performs.

What does this audience appreciation tell us about exceptional performance? What I believe it shows is that there is significant fluctuation around what we are calling standards of excellence. Each cheering moment is an acknowledgment that *this* person and her canine partner, at *this* particular point in time, is realizing success relative to who they are and what they are trying to do, given the challenges of physical mobility, inexperience of the handler, or the temperament of the dog—shy or over-aroused—and so on. Perhaps

Two. Exceptional Performance

the cheering reflects that excellence can be "understood to exist in many different shapes and appear in many different forms" (Kretchmar 2019, 372–73). In other words, we allow that there are different standards of excellence that apply to different categories of agility practitioners. After all, no one would deny that some professional women golfers achieve excellence even though they may not drive the ball as far down the fairway compared to professional men golfers. It makes sense to say that excellence may apply within each category of athlete, allowing for exceptional performance to be attributed equally to men and women athletes. In agility there is no difference in skillfulness between men and women as handlers. It is a bit like equestrian show jumping, eventing, and dressage, where men and women compete against one another in the same classes and divisions. So in these cases the standard of excellence applies equally across gender.

But not all differences between practitioners are irrelevant to skillfulness. Consider the aging agility handler who totters around the course, sometimes falling down (I've done this). Consider the young dog in training or the shy dog who is paralyzed by the vast and seemingly frightening competitive agility ring.

Why not specify a standard of exceptional performance that shows equal respect for these differences? Even if we believe that there should be different standards of excellence for different categories of athletes, how can we possibly clarify these standards and the different degrees of exceptional performance within each category? For example, should we allow that older or less physically capable handlers get more time on the course? And what would count as an excellent, an average, or a poor performance within the senior handler division? How do we decide who should be allowed to enter this category, especially since age does not necessarily reflect physical conditioning? Moreover, if we allow that standards of excellence fluctuate across categories of athletes, some might argue that we are, in effect, surrendering the "discriminating benchmarks" for exceptional performance (Kretchmar 2015, 373). In other words, more athletes will be considered excellent but at the expense of cheapening the meaning of excellence as the realization of exceptional performance and thereby diminishing the worth of the accomplishments of elite athletes. I will not try to answer these difficult questions about the fluctuating standards of excellence because there is a more serious challenge to the view that excellence is measured by exceptional performance in general.

What Does Luck Have to Do with It?

We have already talked about how luck (bad or good) may skew a particular qualifying run score for a variety of reasons: judging error, distractions from outside the ring, or a slip of a paw on wet grass, for example. In these cases most observers are able to recognize that, under slightly different circumstances, the run would have been exceptional. So our judgments about excellence are not altogether threatened by these kinds of examples. But there is another way in which luck may radically interfere with the concept of excellence understood as the realization of exceptional performance.

Look around at your friends at a local trial. Notice that some of us are older or less agile handlers. Some of us have physical limitations regardless of age. Others scramble to pay for entry fees or to get time off from work or to find help with family care-taking duties for the weekend. Some of us may not have access to agility fields and equipment in order to practice. Imagine that my dog is injured and cannot compete. Or suppose I am injured and I cannot train my dog. The most interesting feature of these kinds of impediments is that they are, in one way or another, out of our control. Because we lack control over these genetic and environmental conditions, we might say that our athletic performances, whether exceptional or not, are also at the mercy of this general kind of luck.

These are cases of "constitutive" bad luck,[5] where circumstances impede exceptional performance and interfere with realizing excellence. But the contrary is true as well. For those of us who are *privileged* with respect to age, physical mobility, health, resources, and our dog's temperament, for example, the achievement of exceptional performance is equally shaped by conditions that are in significant ways beyond the control of the agent. Luck of this kind threatens to undermine our ordinary claims about athletes who display

Two. Exceptional Performance

exceptional performance. If athletic success depends on natural ability, and if natural ability is itself shaped by genetic and environmental conditions that are beyond the control of the athlete, then we might suspect that the athlete does not deserve the praise for her success or, for that matter, the blame for failing to succeed.[6]

This surprising and counter-intuitive conclusion has its philosophical origins in what Nagel (1979) and Williams (1981) have called "moral luck." Nagel, for example, identifies four different ways in which luck may interfere with our ordinary moral evaluations of persons and what they do. For our purposes, it is constitutive luck that is relevant. Constitutive luck is described by Nagel (1979, 28) as "the kind of person you are, where this is not just a question of what you deliberately do, but of your inclinations, capacities, and temperament." More specifically,

> constitutive luck is luck in who one is, or in the traits and dispositions that one has. Since our genes, care-givers, peers, and other environmental influences all contribute to making us who we are (and since we have no control over these) it seems that who we are is at least largely a matter of luck. Since how we act is partly a function of who we are, the existence of constitutive luck entails that what actions we perform depends on luck too [Nelkin 2023].

Once we acknowledge that constitutive luck positions agility handlers and their dogs differently, allowing some a genetic and environmental advantage and others a disadvantage, then exceptional performance comes to seem *less* exceptional. This is so because what is achieved—the success—cannot be wholly credited to the agility team itself. In other words, in a fundamental sense excellence is not earned, deserved, or praiseworthy since it is largely the outcome of accidental and fortuitous circumstances that handlers and their dogs cannot control such as age, mobility, resources, health, our dog's temperament, and so on.

Moral luck is a serious paradox for moral appraisals of people and what they do. Taken to its logical extreme, no one is ever morally responsible, praiseworthy or blameworthy for any action. In this way causal determinism threatens our very intuitive idea about persons as agents who act freely. Nagel (1976, 37) puts the point this way:

Canine Agility and the Meaning of Excellence

I believe that in a sense the problem has no solution, because something in the idea of agency is incompatible with actions being events, or people being things. But as the external determinants of what someone has done are gradually exposed, in their effect on consequences, character, and choice itself, it becomes gradually clear that actions are events and people things. Eventually nothing remains which can be ascribed to the responsible self, and we are left with nothing but a portion of the larger sequence of events, which can be deplored or celebrated, but not blamed or praised.

It is not surprising that the paradox of moral luck has migrated into the philosophy of sport where athletic success is typically attributed to an athlete's natural ability and hard work.[7] What can we say to mitigate the problem and, perhaps, salvage the idea that excellence is exceptional performance?

"Matters of Fortune"

Consider this bad luck story. In early March 2023 Maggie and I did a run-through at a local indoor equestrian arena that our agility club rents one day a week during the winter and spring. She ran fast and enthusiastically as usual. But when I got home I could see that she was not walking or trotting evenly. A few days off, then an off-leash romp on the third day assured me that the limp was gone; she seemed fine. Still, I was cautious about agility class that week by trying to do about half of our usual time and effort in the ring. Fast forward one month and to two more episodes of limping. The last just brought me to tears since her practice at the indoor arena—two brief but fast runs—created so much soreness that she could hardly bear weight on her left front leg. I won't belabor the details of our visits to the vet and the cautious route to recovery we began from that moment. But let me say something about how my world changed. Agility is at the center of things for me: practicing handling skills, short training sessions in public parks, agility classes and workshops, interacting with friends who have agility dogs, planning for competitions, and going to competitions. Because I have only one dog in training, the very possibility that Maggie would not ever be healthy

Two. Exceptional Performance

enough to continue agility work was a deep, deep disappointment. I know it seems overly dramatic, but I wondered how I could continue to take pleasure or satisfaction from anything whatsoever without agility in my life.

For Aristotle, a flourishing human life is one that contains activities, friends, good health, and projects that extend into the future. Conditions like these, what Aristotle calls "external goods," make life inherently valuable; they are among the necessary ingredients of a good life. But because they cannot be controlled by the agent, a good life is made vulnerable to reversals or changes of circumstances.[8] A flourishing life in my case includes these activities that cluster around agility. It won't be the same for other people, of course, who form attachments to different kinds of projects and activities. Maggie's lameness is a perfect example of how external events outside of my control diminished and impeded an activity that makes my life meaningful and valuable. Moreover, if excellence in agility depends on the *success* of exceptional performance, then likewise it is made vulnerable by the vicissitudes of external conditions that are not controlled by handlers and their dogs. This seems to suggest that the concept of excellence, understood in this particular way, is untenable. How can we possibly celebrate brilliant performances in agility and praise athletes for their successes if these performances are at the mercy of conditions that are uncontrollable, unpredictable, and unreliable?

Aristotle's own view about the role of luck in a flourishing life is nuanced and sophisticated. While Aristotle does believe that reversals of fortune can interfere with or impede a good life, it is only in extreme conditions that we will say that an agent is not living a good life. These will be cases where misfortune is considerable and extends over long periods of time. In these instances a person's opportunities to live a flourishing life are thwarted and impaired. Significant bad fortune can interfere with the activities necessary to live well. But small strokes of good or bad fortune will not disrupt a good life if the moral character of a person is stable and enduring.

> However, many events are matters of fortune, and some are smaller, some greater. Hence, while small strokes of good or ill fortune clearly

will not influence his life, many great strokes of good fortune will make it more blessed, since in themselves they naturally add adornment to it, and his use of them proves to be fine and excellent. Conversely, if they are great misfortunes, they oppress and spoil his blessedness, since they involve pain and impede many activities.... And since it is activities that control life, as we said, no blessed person could ever become miserable, since he will never do hateful and base actions. For a truly good and intelligent person, we suppose, will bear strokes of fortune suitably, and from his resources at any time will do the finest actions, just as a good general will make the best use of his forces in war, and a good shoemaker will produce the finest shoe from the hides given him, and similarly for all other craftsmen [Aristotle 1985, 1100b20–1101a13].

Aristotle offers a way out of the problem of moral luck in sport. He does so by reminding us that successful activities are indeed necessary for an excellent human life and, while these activities are vulnerable to "strokes of good and ill fortune," what can remain stable and enduring is the moral character of the person who suffers from the variability of luck. In other words, the weight-bearing load for value is the person and her moral qualities rather than the success of the activities she performs. This does not make the success or failure of these activities irrelevant or unimportant, but it locates the excellent part in closer proximity to the person and, presumably, to those qualities of character that she can be held responsible for acquiring and sustaining.

In a similar way we are now in a position to reevaluate the idea that excellence in agility is the *success* of exceptional performance. Perhaps Carr (2002, 203) was on the right track when he suggested that both winners and losers in sport deserve our praise for the qualities of their character such as courage, self-control, and fair-mindedness. These qualities, he believes, are not subject to the mercy of the genetic and environmental lottery so, according to Carr, we can hold athletes responsible and praiseworthy for displaying these traits in sport.[9]

Introducing Sue Pietricola

I spoke with Sue Pietricola about her dogs, how she got started doing agility, and what she believes it means to display excellence in

Two. Exceptional Performance

Sue Pietricola's dog, Seamus, drives out of the tunnel. Sue Pietricola's agility field, Grand Isle, Vermont, July 2019 (photograph by S. Pietricola).

agility. Sue got her interest in agility from riding horses. But when she started with Corgis in 1995, she became a fan of the sport. Her expertise in the practice field and in competitive trialing has been honed by owning and training many Corgis: Rugby, Griffin, Thisby, and Seamus, to name a few. Compared to obedience, she said, "agility was such a breath of fresh air. Okay, so this is where the dog is supposed to go. And you can accomplish that in a host of different ways. So you have all these variables, and there's a playfulness to that. And then when you do it wrong, you still learn something from it, which is a good thing. But when you do it right, it's like, wow, it all comes together and it feels great."

What Does Excellence in Agility Look Like?

Well, this is my whole thing about excellence, okay? Excellence is a made-up thing that we have in our heads, and we all have some sort of little image of what we think that looks like. But for every dog and every human being and every dog–human being combo on the planet, excellence looks like something different. So if I see a person who's new to agility and they go out there and they accomplish something new, and they have that "I did it!" look on their face, and if it was a stretch for them, then to me that's excellence.

What I'm looking for is what some people call "being in the zone," where you're present in the moment. You're not thinking about, like, "Oh, my God, I just screwed this up back there." You're present in the moment, you're together, you're in sync and you're understanding each other and you're both doing your very best job. I think it gets back to where you are in this journey. What does excellence look like for this team, this dog, this partnership, on this day, under these circumstances? For example, suppose a nearby train comes through while you are in the middle of competitive run. And maybe you have a sensitive dog and your dog manages to stay with you and stay connected even though he could have potentially run out of the ring. Anything that you have worked hard to achieve, and you achieve it, is excellence. But really, excellence is being in the zone. I'm looking for the drug of being in the zone which is when you're totally connected and present in the moment. You're not thinking about what happened before or the future. You have a plan for the future, but you're in the present.

Summary

This chapter focuses exclusively on the idea that excellence in agility is the realization of exceptional performance. But what we found is some unclarity about what it means to display exceptional performance. We considered the qualifying run score as a measure of excellence, but the standards for qualifying runs are variable across agility organizations with little or no justification for accepting one standard over another. This implies that the concept of excellence itself fluctuates with little or no justification. It also seems possible that there may be particular displays of exceptional performance

Two. Exceptional Performance

Sue Pietricola's dog, Thisby, is showing nice form over this jump. Sue Pietricola's agility field, Grand Isle, Vermont, July 2019 (photograph by S. Pietricola).

that are not qualifying runs as well as particular qualifying runs that are not displays of exceptional performance. If this is possible then we should look elsewhere for a more reliable guide to what counts as exceptional performance.

Displays of exceptional performance may be more finely individuated by skills that are specific to the sport of agility. I've called these tiny, beautiful moments to distinguish this kind of performance from a qualifying run per se. These skills are varied and numerous for both handlers and dogs. At the very least we expect that dogs display their understanding of correctly negotiating the equipment in agility, their understanding of when to focus on the handler, and when to focus on the obstacles, and that they are responsive to body cues and verbal cues while running at speed. For handlers we acknowledge the skill of watching your dog, cuing the obstacle early, and finding the best path for the dog through the course. Together the agility team

Canine Agility and the Meaning of Excellence

will display mutual trust, teamwork, and communication, even if this exceptional performance is momentary and fleeting.

But even this more promising interpretation of exceptional performance is dubious in the face of constitutive luck. The concept of excellence under review depends on the *success* of exceptional performance. But whether or not an agility team achieves success is contingent on a variety of conditions that she cannot control: age, mobility, health, and resources such as time and money, the dog's temperament, and so on. Because success is so fundamentally dependent on these features of genetic and environmental luck, we cannot reasonably attribute praise or deservingness to the athletic team for their displays of exceptional performance. This outcome is unsatisfactory. What I believe it reveals is that the concept of excellence understood as the achievement of exceptional performance is not defensible. We *do* want to praise agility teams for their excellence! Fortunately, there are other plausible candidates for what it means to realize excellence in agility. In the next chapter we consider excellence as displays of moral character and the excellence inherent to "playing the game" of agility.

Three

Agility as Play

> *The "serendipitous model of sport" ... takes its primary values from the worlds of play and spirituality* (Kretchmar 2015, 88).

In the last chapter we found reasons for doubting the plausibility of the view that excellence in agility is the achievement of exceptional performance. I do not believe that these reasons definitively undermine performance exceptionalism. But they are certainly sufficient to inspire us to look beyond this view for a rival candidate. Still, the idea that excellence is exceptional achievement is a difficult position to relinquish. Many practitioners of the sport aspire to this kind of accomplishment measured by points, titles, and championships. And even moderately successful competitors like myself are enamored by this ideal to enter even more competitive agility events and to invest even more time, energy, and emotional heft in order to sustain that success. But sometimes even avid competitors can be startled out of this pursuit.

Agility Is Not Just Something We Do on the Side[1]

On Friday, September 13, 2019, my beautiful Australian Shepherd, Maggie, went missing. Maggie is my best friend—the love of my life—and my agility partner. Imagine receiving a call from 3,000 miles away that the gate to our fenced yard was found open and she is gone. Imagine being the dog sitter and having to make that call to an owner. We were both in tears, our hearts just stricken.

Canine Agility and the Meaning of Excellence

My husband and I were in California attending the wedding of my son. We left Maggie in the excellent care of our trainer's daughter who was staying at our house but at work that afternoon. She is responsible, accomplished, smart, and professional. She was not negligent or forgetful. She did nothing wrong. But we soon learned that Maggie was not just missing. She was stolen from our yard using a black web short leash with a clip that secured the gate of our chain link fence. We discovered that the leash was gone when we returned home.

Of all the things we did to locate her (and there were many, many things), the most important turned out to be our appeals to dog-loving members of our community through Facebook pages, some devoted to lost and found pets. Within several days the story of "Missing Dog—Maggie" had gone viral with more than 1,000 posts and shares. When I walked downtown to distribute posters, Maggie's story was already known. The clerk behind the desk at the post office tearfully took Maggie's picture and identifying information and promised to place it where all the carriers could see. Our local paper had already heard the news when they agreed to interview me for a story. Dog groomers, vets, and dog control officers from all over the North Country had seen her picture on Facebook. The officer from our city police department who was assigned to my case had seen that she was missing and supposed stolen. Just so you know, I am not all that "connected" with social media. But it seems Maggie was. I think it was because this event hit a nerve. Dogs sometimes go missing because they escape from yards or cars. They go missing also when they grow old and infirm and die a natural death. But stealing a dog from a backyard? We know this happens, of course. But our community would not stand for it.

At this point in my life I have lost both my parents. We have had to put our previous dogs to sleep for one reason or another. But there is nothing to compare to what it was like to lose Maggie in this particular way. I felt as if my heart had been literally torn out. Not one thing in my professional or personal life mattered anymore. And I genuinely believed that I would never be happy or joyous again. Was she hungry or scared? Was someone mistreating her? Was she in another state by now? When we returned home after three days,

Three. Agility as Play

I was even more stricken to see all her toys in the house and in the yard. Maggie steals one of my socks every once in a while and carries it around the house to get my attention. She never chews it up; she just lets me know that she has something of mine. So when I saw that she had taken my sock halfway down the hall and left it there, I let out a wail of inconsolable anguish.

Two different possible sightings of my dog placed her within two blocks of us on either side. Both people called in these sightings to me and to our city police department. But was this reliable information? It was hard to know. I received a lot of weird calls that week. One woman horrified me by reporting that a few years ago a ring of thieves was taking dogs from backyards to use them for fighting other dogs. When I learned the actual address of one of these possible sightings in our neighborhood, I decided (after another tearful, sleepless night) that I would drive down to this house and secretly park nearby in the early morning to see if the residents brought her outside to do her business. "I don't think that's such a great idea," my husband Chuck said. He was worried that if I did see her I would jump out and confront the dog thief to get her back. "I won't! I promise to speed-dial Officer Kowalowski the minute I get a glimpse of her." He was not convinced. And Chuck had good reason to suspect I was not thinking clearly. I hadn't slept or eaten much for about six days at this point.

In any case, I didn't see Maggie that morning on my ill-advised "stake out." The police officer I contacted later told me that they had already visited that residence and hadn't seen her. But there was some encouraging news. A local woman had been arrested for shoplifting at Kinney Drugs nearby. When she was interviewed, she claimed to have two addresses (her mother's residence and her boyfriend's house) which, coincidentally, corresponded with the two sightings of Maggie! The police officer who interviewed the shoplifter put it together and suspected this woman to have Maggie in her possession. As hard as it was, I impatiently waited until they followed up with interviews and scrutinized an on-street video camera that revealed this particular woman walking Maggie on a street two blocks from our house.

Before an arrest was made, seven days after Maggie was stolen, I

Canine Agility and the Meaning of Excellence

received multiple phone messages and texts from our neighbor, our dog-sitter, and the police department. Maggie had been returned to our yard sometime in the morning after we left for work. The gate was closed. When our neighbors heard her bark (!), they rushed over to wait for our return and to babysit. A small crowd of people in our immediate circle of friends was gathered in our backyard to watch over Maggie until we could get there. It is not possible to explain how I felt. I have never been so overcome with gratefulness. She was a little shy but unhurt. Her beautiful Aussie coat had been hacked off with scissors, leaving large blunt marks in her fur. And she had white paint spots all over her back. But I didn't care; she was home.

The word spread like wildfire. We contacted new Facebook friends and colleagues, emailed and telephoned family. Neighbors stopped us in the street and spoke across our backyard fence to express their relief and pleasure that she was safe and back with her family. The clerks at the post office phoned at 8:00 a.m. the next day just to confirm that she was home and safe! When Chuck stopped at Mickeys, our neighborhood bar and pizza establishment, the bartenders rushed out from behind the bar to shake hands and clap him on the back. Two people sitting at the bar who Chuck did not even know exclaimed excitedly, "Maggie's back? Oh, how wonderful!" The vets and the staff at our veterinary hospital, the groomer who scheduled Maggie immediately to be trimmed, and the pet food owner who printed a free id tag for her collar all were invested in this event. It seemed they each had a stake in the outcome that was authentic and heartfelt. There was a lot of crying and hugging those first days that she was home.

There are a few things that have stuck with me since then. First is a new humbleness about what really matters. I am so truly grateful for all the concern, help, and even anguish that my friends experienced when this happened. This extends to the many people who I never met directly but who shared posts, looked for Maggie around town, put up posters, and expressed their support in one way or another.

And now I want to say why I am really writing this down for others to read. It is my realization that doing agility with Maggie has positioned me in a community that has become precious and dear to

Three. Agility as Play

me. By far, my friends who were most stricken by Maggie's theft and those who responded immediately with their time, energy and concern were my trainer and all of my agility classmates that I have gotten to know over the last two years.[2] Sometimes this took the form of a simple email: "I'm so sorry. I just can't imagine how you feel." Others busily printed flyers and posted them around town. And then, when we returned to agility class just one week later, it was like *I* had come home. Because what I realized during that awful, wrenching week without Maggie was that all of these people and their dogs were at the center of my life. We have cheered each other on at workshops and seminars, in classes, and at trials. We have walked ridiculously hard courses that our trainer has set, laughing and shaking our heads about how unlikely it would be to actually remember the sequence. We have been challenged and encouraged by our intrepid trainer who is both a coach and a friend. And then it seemed we were so collectively sad about Maggie. And so very overjoyed to be all reunited again.

So my message is this. Agility is not *just* something I do on the side. It's true that I have a job, a husband, and other pleasures that I value. But I know what is at the center of things now. I know what I look forward to in the day. I know what I think about when I drift off to sleep. I know what will focus my attention and bring out my competitive spirit. It is trying to excel at an incredibly challenging sport, together as a team with a smart and sometimes difficult dog, in a community of friends who are as serious and as devoted to this activity as I am. During those seven days without Maggie I felt stricken, bereft, like my heart had been ripped apart. But I came to understand that this loss was actually larger and deeper. Losing Maggie also carved out a hole in my life that was normally filled with agility training, agility classes, conversation about agility, and, most of all, companionship with those people and their dogs that make up this precious community to which I now belong. We shouldn't have to lose our dogs for even a day to realize and to appreciate this most profound truth: agility is not just something we do on the side. It makes us whole. It makes life coherent and meaningful.

This poignant description of the role of agility in my life reveals something that I may have forgotten in my recent competitive labors. And that is the possibility that the measure of excellence in agility is located somewhere outside of the realization of exceptional achievement. In this vignette there is no mention about successful qualifying runs or even tiny, beautiful moments of teamwork, communication, and brilliance between handler and dog. Rather, my story about losing Maggie profiles bad luck (losing her) and good luck (finding her), how an activity like agility can be a meaningful and necessary ingredient of a good life, how the absence of this activity can impair such a life, and the central role of friends in a like-minded community of agility enthusiasts. This chapter is devoted to exploring some of these alternative conceptions of the value of excellence in agility. Specifically, there are two views that we will explore:

- Excellence is located in the moral virtues of questing rather than exceptional achievement.
- Excellence is located in the play relation between handler and dog.

Moral Virtues

Remember the story about Rob and Dusty? Even though Rob is thoroughly committed to making Dusty into a champion agility dog, success eludes him again and again. But what we should really notice about this story is what moral qualities Rob displays in his struggle: persistence, grit, resilience, constancy, and effort. "I remind myself that the whole point of this agility adventure is to shake off that shroud of timorousness and restraint. To be bold, to be heroic, to strive and achieve. I need it, Dusty needs it—it's high time we went out there and just *did* it" (Rodi 2009, 77).

Rob's moral character is on display throughout his struggles in the competitive agility ring. Yet this quality of will or intention is not unique to Rob and to his particular pursuit of glory in the sport of agility. For example, Schmid (2017, 38–40) makes "self-fulfilling golf" the centerpiece of his analysis of the game of golf, where the golfer aims to cultivate certain qualities that better oneself and not merely his or her game. To motivate such

Three. Agility as Play

a view Schmid argues that a "fix-it mentality" approach to playing the game is merely instrumental. This is the psychological state of the golfer who plays solely to achieve an outcome, like a good score, winning a match, or looking good. But this approach is misguided, according to Schmid, because it fails to fully realize the larger context of the game and its potential for more formative experiences of those who play.

> Golf as a practice has to be set within a larger context of personal aspiration and meaning, if the player is to retain a fulfilling experience in it. The life and its virtues must supersede the outcome, if the golfer is to hold on to his love of the game, and the meaning that he brings to his play [Schmid 2017, 43].

According to Schmid, the particular moral and intellectual virtues that can be cultivated by players of golf include:

> courage, commitment, and freedom;
> temperament, artfulness, and beauty;
> justice, identity, and community;
> wisdom, self-knowledge, and truth; and
> friendship, meaning, and self-fulfillment.

There is quite a bit more to Schmid's analysis of "self-fulfilling golf." I'm not sure we need all of these details in order to identify what is largely correct and helpful in his analysis as well as how this concept falls short of explaining excellence in agility.

Significantly, when Schmid recommends cultivating the moral and intellectual virtues of the athlete he is recommending a way to approach and to play the game of golf. But he is also appealing to a foundational sense of excellence owed to Aristotle. This Aristotelian account of human excellence directs the athlete to become a certain kind of person, in general, and directs her to live a certain kind of life, a flourishing life. Hence, success in playing the game of golf or any sport does not depend on realizing exceptional achievement. For this reason, it is less vulnerable to what we have called moral luck. The responsibility lies with the athlete herself to develop these traits of character. Schmid's analysis of "self-fulfilling golf" is an instance of Kretchmar's (2015, 88)

Canine Agility and the Meaning of Excellence

"serendipitous model of sport." "This model takes its primary values from the worlds of play and spirituality. It seeks temporary relief from the normalcy, obligations, predictability, and meritocracy of work.... It generates hope based on grace or other factors that are not entirely under one's control."

I can easily imagine myself aspiring to excellence by cultivating the moral and intellectual virtues that emerge from playing golf. I like the game and maybe I could even come to love it. For others this may be possible for soccer, basketball, ultimate Frisbee, billiards, badminton, tennis, or football. But one sport that cannot be explained by this account of excellence is agility. The reason is that human participants are essentially intertwined with canine participants. There is just no agility without the dog. So while I might well cultivate the moral and intellectual virtues by practicing agility, this seems to leave out the very heart of the sport.

The exact characterization of this relationship between handler and dog is fascinating and complex. We will have more to say about training and communication in Chapter Six. But for now I offer these remarks that attempt to capture the nature of the bond between a human handler and her canine performance partner. What kind of relationship is this? It is not training dogs per se but training *with* dogs (Haraway 2003). This involves a "mutual, cooperative, reciprocal process of education in which the human is not the only agent" (Lund 2014, 107). Agility does not serve any particular pragmatic purpose, but it invites an "opportunity for joy and a flourishing relationship with a significant other."

These remarks imply that teamwork with a canine partner is not accidental to the sport. The dog is not just an add-on piece of equipment like a golf club, a tennis racket, or a basketball. The dog has agency of a kind that is essential to the fundamental nature of agility. Consequently, any account of excellence that fails to include this feature will be necessarily incomplete. As handlers (i.e., human beings) we might well try to cultivate intellectual and moral virtue while practicing agility; this undertaking is certainly possible and is maybe even desirable. But ultimately the moral character of the handler by itself will be an imperfect measure of excellence in the sport of agility.

Three. Agility as Play

Playing Agility

If we are looking for a way to profile the exquisite and complex bond between a handler and her agility canine partner, a good place to start is by characterizing this relationship as *playing* with your

JoLee Yeddo comforts her Standard Schnauzer, Arya. Agility Dogs of the Adirondacks Trial in Elizabethtown, New York, July 2023 (artsyfartsyphotosbyshanon.com).

Canine Agility and the Meaning of Excellence

dog. Recall what Kretchmar (2015, 88) says about the "serendipitous model of sport." "This model takes its primary values from the worlds of play and spirituality. It seeks temporary relief from the normalcy, obligations, predictability, and meritocracy of work." So what does play look like in the agility setting? Let me describe some true scenarios I have witnessed, names withheld.

Playing Frisbee with dog A: Suppose I am playing Frisbee with dog A. I get her excited, throw the Frisbee, and I tell her to "get it." Maybe she runs after the Frisbee, maybe not. Maybe she decides to sniff for a bone in the yard instead. Or maybe she decides to run the fence line to chase another dog walking down the sidewalk.

Throwing toys in the practice ring with dog B: Consider dog B and his handler who are practicing in agility class. The handler throws the ball on the dog's line after B successfully enters and exits a tunnel. Dog B scampers after the ball and races around the ring with the ball in his mouth for about five to seven minutes. Nothing can induce him to give it up.

Get ready to run with dog C: A handler proceeds to set up dog C at the start line of a practice run. First the handler engages C by tugging to the start line. C pulls ferociously, growling and leaping. When the handler says "give," C instantly releases the toy and sits between the handler's legs facing the first obstacle.

Clearly there is not just one way of "playing agility." In the first example, the handler of dog A is just suggesting some ways of engaging in play when she throws the Frisbee. If A does not respond to this suggestion, then the handler might try another toy or even food to engage her dog. If I'm just *playing* with my dog, it doesn't matter, right? But importantly, A has not done anything wrong or violated any rule about play because in this case there is no standard of play; there is no expectation or demand to which A must conform. This example is consistent with remarks made by Ralf Weber from Happy Dog Training. Weber is the author of an article titled "Play Is the Way." Here Weber identifies six different key elements in play: searching, stalking, chasing, fighting, celebrating, and consuming. If your dog likes to chase, then the best kinds of games will be those where he can run after a ball or Frisbee. Sometimes a dog prefers to consume food as part of the game, etc. Additionally, your dog may be either a "supportive" player or a "competitive" player. A supportive player is likely to bring the ball back for another round of fetch; a competitive player will prefer the struggle of tugging. The main recommendation by Mr. Weber is to find out what kind of play your dog prefers and then to design games he enjoys. This information about play is mostly descriptive. In other words, there is no suggestion about *how one should* play with your dog beyond the general instruction to find out what kinds of games your particular dog prefers and use those.

Dog B scampers around the agility practice ring with a ball, overjoyed by the reward for a good tunnel send. In this case, when the handler throws the ball it means something. It is not a random attempt to interact with dog B. My agility instructor, Robin Magee, has taught many, many young dogs and puppies in foundation classes at Aussie Acres Agility over the years. I never quite appreciated how central playing is to the sport until I watched her start two of her own puppies in agility foundation skills. Robin introduces each new skill as a game that promises a treat or toy reward (tug toy, Frisbee, ball)—from crate training to walking a plank, running through a tunnel, weave entries, and "go" lines. The main idea is that if you (dog) want to play with me, do this little activity first. The refrain is always to reward a skill performed well. So there is a standard of play operating in this case unlike throwing the Frisbee to dog A in the backyard example. Pretty soon the obstacles themselves become rewarding to most dogs. But the toy is always at hand whenever your dog needs more reinforcement for training a particular skill. Dog B probably understands the reward for the tunnel, but because B runs wildly around with the ball for a while, the skill acquisition is a truncated version of what we should expect in later stages of training.

Now consider the case with dog C. The first thing you may think when you see this team practice and compete is that you are witnessing a routine that is familiar and comfortable for both handler and dog. The tugging looks initially frightening. Wow, such high energy directed at a toy and, of course, a start line. But in an instant the toy is dropped and the focus shifts forward to the first obstacle, and all that energy surges through the dog to run the course. In her blog post "Play Before Work," Bad Dog Agility instructor Sarah

Canine Agility and the Meaning of Excellence

Fernandezlopez recommends tugging as a way of reinforcing the training of agility dogs, but what you are aiming for initially must be created in stages, beginning with a "happy, interactive, and physical" play relation. She suggests that later in agility training the tugging will become more structured so that the dog will bite the toy on cue, release on cue, and retrieve the toy in the presence of distractions. For dog C there is a standard of play operating and it is one that the dog has learned throughout many iterations of the same type of scenario.

What Is Play?

Although there is considerable literature in the philosophy of sport about play, games, and sport, I like the straightforward distinction made by Suits (2002). Suits differentiates between "primitive play" and "sophisticated play." The best example of primitive play is to imagine a baby playing in the bathwater, splashing herself and her bath-giver joyfully. According to Suits, we can define this kind of play in a negative way. The baby is not working, nor is she engaged in any instrumental enterprise (bathing herself or helping her parent). Is the baby acting randomly or without purpose? No. Splashing in the water is pleasing. There is the delightful experience as positive feedback, so she continues to splash. Although there may be skills that develop out of this moment, "the skills learned are not the payoff the baby is seeking" (Suits 2002, 30).

> Primitive play, I suggest, is not concerned primarily with the exercise and enjoyment of skills but with the introduction of new experiences that arise, usually, serendipitously. Still, the repetition of these experiences may very well result in the development of skills directed toward the recurrence of those experiences, and such skills may, although they need not, come to be valued for their own sake. When that *does* happen we are just beginning to move from primitive play to sophisticated play, that is, to games, and perhaps to something else as well.

If we applied Suits' distinction between primitive and sophisticated play to dogs A, B, and C, no doubt he would describe dog A as engaged in primitive play. Retrieving the Frisbee, chasing a squirrel, or running the fence line in pursuit of a skateboarder is enjoyed just for the experience and delight of each of these activities. Suits might describe dog B as moving beyond primitive play to something like sophisticated play, where the skill of negotiating obstacles on an agility course are just emerging from the immediate reward for going through a tunnel. And we may speculate about dog C. C's behavior, tugging at the start line, giving up the toy, and beginning the sequence of obstacles, indicates skillful performance. The dog clearly understands the role of playing with the toy and understands the criteria for correctly engaging in this activity. So perhaps Suits would say that this is an instance of sophisticated play where the skills are acquired and employed in order to be used in the activity of running an agility sequence.

There is another sense in which agility is associated with play, and that is when the activity is characterized, in general, as playing a game. For example, consider how Tammy Moody (2018) describes how to *practice* playing agility. In her article "For Play's Sake," Moody declares that playing games with your dog should not be just another training exercise; "it should be play for the sake of play." The definition of play used here is "to engage in an activity for enjoyment and recreation rather than a serious or practical purpose." Moody recommends a number of practical tips for engaging in agility play, including identifying what kinds of play your dog likes, being attentive to your dog's space, moving or running to create playful situations, and transitioning out of play to signal the end of a play session. But the most revealing comment emerges at the end of the article when Moody (2018, 42) claims that "agility is one big game—one we play with our dogs."

> If we become the pushy kid or the bully, the controlling one with all the rules, and the one who becomes upset when the rules aren't followed, then our dogs will learn to avoid us or play the game because they have been forced to instead of being a choice.... When we create play that is about play, and when we make the game about the game and not about the dog or ourselves, we have a much better chance of gaining our dog's attention.

Excellent Play

Reflect on Moody's comment that as handlers we should avoid becoming "the pushy kid or the bully, the controlling one with all the rules, and the one who becomes upset when the rules aren't followed." This is a curious remark. If agility is a game that is played with your dog, and the handler does not use and apply rules for playing the game (leaving aside the "bully" attitude), then there is no particular measure for excellence in agility. This cannot be right. In order to identify excellence in agility there must be a way of differentiating genuine instances of excellence from those that do not count as excellent. In other words, there must be criteria for excellence. For example, in Chapter Two, when we characterized excellence as exceptional performance, the criteria for excellence was the display of skills specific to agility for both handler and dog. And in this chapter, when we identified excellence in agility with the moral character of the handler, the criteria for excellence was the handler's cultivation of moral and intellectual virtues. But what are the criteria for excellence when agility is defined as playing a game with your dog?

The real question we should ask about whether or not agility is a game we play with our dogs is *why* the game is being played. For example, I've observed agility club members who attend run-throughs and who declare that they are "just playing." These dogs might go up the A-frame or they might go in a tunnel. The owner cheers no matter the performance, using no cues or cues that are unclear. These teams frolic around throwing balls and Frisbees, and sometimes what they do is an approximation of the skills we are trying to train and learn in agility classes. But if this is the game that you and your dog choose to play, then the agility ring, including all the equipment, is inconsequential to the activity. You might as well use a soccer field or a dog park to engage in this kind of play with your dog. Following Suits, we might classify this kind of playing as *primitive play* if the motivations for playing are primarily in order to have a delightful experience with your dog.

In the very same ring are those people who are training contact performance. This might involve proofing the pause on the bottom of the down ramp of the dogwalk, using toys and exciting distractions to test the dog's commitment to staying in 2 on 2 off position until the dog is released to the next obstacle. There is a game being played here as well, but it is not only for fun or pleasure. There is a standard of excellence this team is trying to meet and a level of gravity that any observer can see. Contrary to what Moody suggests, there is a serious purpose to the activity (though it may not be done for a practical purpose). And it seems to me also that the activity is not always or necessarily done for reasons of "enjoyable recreation." Perhaps a better description is that the activity of training the dogwalk or the weave poles may be a gradual move from primitive play to sophisticated play, one that involves the development of skills for negotiating obstacles consistent with performance criteria. Not everyone who plays in the agility ring aims for this skill development. Perhaps some dog owners may be entirely happy to splash in the bathwater just for the amusement of the experience.

So, in order for there to be excellence in playing the game of agility there must be, necessarily, the intention to engage in what Suits (2002) calls "sophisticated play." This allows us to specify performance criteria for a variety of skills that eventually develop into the game of agility. Agility practitioners have vastly different reasons for doing agility. But if the activity undertaken points to skill development for the handler or the dog, then this implies that there are standards for performance which, in turn, makes it possible to achieve excellence.

Amateurs Play, Professionals Excel

Why does the issue about *playing agility* matter to excellence? Even though most agility practitioners intend to engage in "sophisticated play," their motivations might best be described as doing the sport "for the love of it." What this suggests is that agility practitioners are better classified as amateurs rather than professionals since professionals value an activity primarily for the payoff or reward that the activity is expected to provide, such as a salary (Suits 2002, 36). For example, this agility coach strongly disavows that agility is a professional pursuit.

Canine Agility and the Meaning of Excellence

> And please don't give me the examples of professional athletes! My dogs are *not* professional athletes. They're just three happy dogs that like to play. *Professional athletes train six days a week, two times a day, for several hours. My dogs train two to three times a week for five to ten minutes...* [Ikonen 2017, 14].

To call agility a sport practiced by an amateur has all kinds of fascinating connotations. One possibility is that amateur agility practitioners do not aim for excellence nor do they successfully achieve excellence. LaVaque-Manty (2009, 143) writes, for example, that "the notion of excellence is relatively straightforward. In sports, there are reasonably clear measures of excellence, of ranking participants, of measuring relative success by straightforward objective measures of achievement. Competitors aim to do as well as possible and ultimately to win." But she adds that in recreational sports people aren't trying to win per se. They undertake these sports for health, for charity, to have fun with friends, etc. So if agility is a sport practiced by amateurs and done "for the love of it," can we expect demonstrations of excellence? LaVaque-Manty (2009, 145) thinks not.

> A figure skater's quadruple jump is praiseworthy precisely because it is so difficult for anyone to accomplish, and no matter how much I train, I will not merit similar appreciation if I can't even get off the ice. Sometimes "A for effort" makes no sense. In fact, while university students who receive B's on assignments frequently lament, "I worked so hard on it," instructors generally and reasonably think "A for effort" was really abandoned as a principle sometime in elementary school. This is all the more true for sports: *just* working hard is not enough for excellence.

Introducing JoLee Yeddo

JoLee Yeddo is a C.P.E. judge and an agility trainer and competitor. She works now as an elementary school teacher. JoLee grew up with dogs. In fact, her father was a canine cop.

JoLee: So the joke around our house was that we were raised by German Shepherds. After I got married, our first dog was a little Miniature Schnauzer. In about 2005–2006, I went to a dog training

Three. Agility as Play

JoLee Yeddo cheers for Arya at the bottom of the A-frame. Agility Dogs of the Adirondacks Trial in Elizabethtown, New York, July 2023 (artsyfartsy-photosbyshanon.com).

club open house in Plattsburgh, and there was this lady there with red hair who said, "You can do agility with your dogs." And I'm like, really? Because I have a Miniature Schnauzer. "Yeah, everybody can do agility with any kind of dog." And I thought that was the coolest thing ever because I thought it was just for people on T.V., people in California and in New York City.

I started going to classes and realized that even my little non-athletic dog actually dug being somewhat athletic. And so we've had Schnauzers ever since. Right now we have a Miniature Schnauzer, a Standard Schnauzer, and a Giant Schnauzer.

Yeah. We like the German dogs. Jeremiah likes the beards. They're just fun. And there's not a lot of them out there. And that makes it fun, too. I like the scruffy dogs. So even a mutt with a beard would be fine. But what I want is a dog that likes to play but has a good work ethic. I'm always looking for a dog with a good sense of

Canine Agility and the Meaning of Excellence

humor because life is too short to take it seriously. Well, they also need a good sense of humor to deal with me.

How do your dogs like agility?

So the ones I have now are fairly new to the sport. The one that we just lost last year took to agility immediately. It was her job and her calling. You could just see that she loved to play this game. My miniature is only two years old. He's brand new. He thinks everything is pretty awesome. And there's snacks after. So it's just great. I mean, I can hear him snorting when he's running the course because he's just having so much fun. He likes the movement and the activity. He's a party animal. He wants to do anything that's fun. And bring snacks.

My older dog likes to finish the game as soon as possible. I think she feels stressed about what she's doing. She still wants to go to the line, though. So as long as she's willing to go to the line with me, we're going to keep playing. But I'm keeping her at a low level and a lower height. That allows her to be successful; she doesn't have to think too hard, and there's a party afterwards every time. She actually moved up into (C.P.E.) level 4, and then she just didn't want to do some of the courses. If I take her to practice, she'll run to the teeter and nail it. She'll run across the dogwalk back and forth and just show off. I mean, she loves it, but in public it's just a little bit scary. So I'm just keeping it simple for her. And as long as she seems happy to go to the line, she gets to keep playing. I mean, I'm not going to push her to get big titles. I like that she's willing to play the sport with me. That's all.

Describe some of your successful moments in the agility ring.

Well, when a run is really successful, and I had a few of these with the Ziva that I have just kept in my mind forever. It's almost like you're watching yourself run from above. It's almost Zen. You're not really thinking about what you're telling them. They understand where we're going and you understand where they're going and there's just no argument about it. It just happens. And you get to the end of the run and it's just like "Wow, that just happened. That was cool." That doesn't happen all the time. With Ziva we got on the same page quite often.

Three. Agility as Play

Now, when things go horribly wrong, you have to be able to laugh at yourself and your dog. Sometimes I make the mistake and send them someplace completely different than where they were supposed to go. And you just have to own it and move on with your day. And sometimes, especially with Schnauzers who are very intelligent, they can be doing things on their own. So sometimes they'll choose a completely different course. And if that happens, you know what? This is a silly sport we play with our dogs. And as long as they're smiling when we get to the end, it's fine. Whatever. We have something to work on and its okay. For example, I had one run with Tyrion, the Miniature Schnauzer, where he ran five dogwalk obstacles in one standard run. He hit the contact on every single one of them. And he was smiling from ear to ear every single time. I couldn't get him to go into the tunnel that was under the dogwalk. He just kept thinking, "I need to do the dogwalk again because it's fun." We still almost qualified because it was only one off-course obstacle. He just kept doing the same dogwalk, back and forth. But he was thrilled. Every time he hit the contact, I was like "Yeah, buddy, that's it. It's awesome."

When I watch you run with your dogs at a trial, I think, "JoLee is so happy and so are her dogs." It's just so obvious to anyone watching.

That's the goal. I mean, if we haven't worked out the quirks and we don't have it ready to trial, that's on me. That's on practice. But at a trial, they want to play with me. So as far as they know, they did it right no matter what.

So you're a C.P.E. judge. Tell us about your job. How did you get started doing that?

Carol Tom was one of the people that I trained with and knew, and she was a key player when I first started agility in C.P.E. I moved to C.P.E. from U.S.D.A.A. because it was more fun and less stressful for me because even though the ribbons don't matter, if you're never getting ribbons, it adds to the stress. It really does. So Carol Tom said to me one day, "You should be a judge." I hadn't really thought of it before then, but she thought it would be a good thing for me. So in order to become a judge, you have to get a CATCH with a dog before you can even apply. Well, my little engine that could was doing really,

really well. And then she actually collapsed in the middle of a run. We were about four Qs away from a CATCH.

We found out that she had congestive heart failure, but I retired her that day. She probably could have earned those last four Qs, but it wasn't worth it to me to put her in danger. So I had to wait for my next dog to be able to earn that. So once we did that in 2016, I went to the judge's training in Michigan. So in 2017 I had three trials where I was under supervision, which was the minimum. And then they let me loose on the world. I love it because I get to travel and I get to see different areas of the country, how they're training their dogs, what they're doing well, what they're not doing well.

So what do you like best about judging?

I love seeing people having fun with their dogs. I've learned a lot about handling and course designing from standing in the middle of the ring. You think you've got a really awesome course, and then you realize while dogs are running it that, no, it could have been better in this spot. You can tweak it, and then reuse it, and then try it later to see if it works better. But you just learn a lot. I like having an open mind. What I find entertaining is to be in the middle of the ring. When handlers mess up, it's fine. But the dogs look at them really funny. From inside the ring you can see the look on their faces close up. Or the dog thought it was something else they were supposed to do. It's just fun.

I've heard some people say that agility is a game that we play with our dogs. So what does that mean to you as a trainer? Can you think of examples?

As a trainer? Yeah. It's definitely a game. Everything should be fun. Things for people are more rewarding if they're fun. And for the dogs it has to be fun too. When they're at the end of the run and their whole body is wriggling or they're jumping, they're hopping, and they're celebrating what they just accomplished with you. "We just did this thing and it was great." And that's why, at the end of the run, whether or not we did it right, I want them to celebrate that we did something together. That was really cool. There's a celebration. There's a game at the end of it. It's not just work.

Well, even when I was an athlete in high school, I had a different mindset than other people. Yeah, we're playing a sport, we're working hard at it, but it should be fun also. And it's not always just about the winning, it's about celebrating the time we're spending out there on the court playing with our friends too. I was not necessarily normal in that respect. But it is just a game. If you compare it with the rest of the things happening in our world, it's kind of silly. I mean, it's an escape from the world somewhat, and it should be fun.

What's the difference between playing the game of agility and throwing a Frisbee for your dog?
Playing Frisbee on the beach is exercise. Maybe not mindful exercise. And it's just back and forth, where the dog is using his body. In agility a dog has to use his brain more than just to catch something in the air. He has to think and to be responsible for knowing the obstacles.

Is it possible to play the game of agility with your dog and *be competitive?*
You're always aiming for excellence, but making it fun at the same time. It's a lot more fun when you Q. Earning points and titles is not everything, although it's fun to work for the titles. It's a challenge. It's about taking it seriously enough without being so serious that you don't like it anymore. Because I've seen people like that too. They're so serious about getting the next Q that they forget that it's supposed to be fun. You can be competitive, but then you can also run the risk of ruining your relationship with your dog by making it all about that. Because they're your partner in this game. Your partner might not be feeling it today. Maybe you have to take up more of the workload. Not every day is going to be perfect.

Summary

If excellence is not the realization of exceptional performance, then what is it? One plausible answer is that excellence is more closely associated with the will or intention to succeed. This idea privileges the moral character of an agility handler who strives for excellence. Grit, determination, resilience, and courage are some of

Canine Agility and the Meaning of Excellence

JoLee Yeddo is having some tunnel fun with her dog, Arya. Agility Dogs of the Adirondacks Trial in Elizabethtown, New York, July 2023 (artsyfartsyphotosbyshanon.com).

the valued traits of character that contribute to human excellence. But human excellence is only part of the story. Any analysis of excellence that leaves out the dog, or reduces the dog to a sporting instrument like a golf club, a tennis racket, or a basketball, is incomplete and misrepresentative of our sport.

In order to capture the meaningful and complex relationship between handler and dog we should instead consider agility as "playing a game with our dog." Here also we must be careful since the concept of play itself is ambiguous. Suits (2002) helpfully distinguishes between "primitive play" and "sophisticated play." Sophisticated play includes skill development and, for this reason, it aligns better with the kind of playing in agility that specifies performance criteria and therefore standards of excellence.

Still there may be a lingering doubt about whether excellence can be achieved by those who play the game of agility. Most of us will

Three. Agility as Play

say that we undertake the sport "for the love of it," for pleasure, for recreation, to spend time with our dogs, or to engage with a social community of like-minded enthusiasts. In other words, we declare ourselves to be amateurs rather than professionals. The hard truth for this population may be that practicing agility for recreational reasons may not necessarily include the realization of excellence. Having fun with our friends at an agility trial isn't actually the same as being excellent. The main question for avid practitioners of the sport of agility is "What are we trying to do?"

Four

Agility as Hobby

> *The true amateur athlete ... is one who takes up sport for the fun of it and the love of it, and to whom success or defeat is a secondary matter so long as the play is good ... it is from doing the thing well, doing the thing handsomely, doing the thing intelligently that one derives the pleasure which is the essence of sport* (William James as quoted in Booth [1999, 50]).

Arnold Lobel's (1980) fable "The Camel Dances" is a poignant story of a camel whose devotion to ballet leads her to practice her "five basic positions a hundred times each day" under the hot desert sun. "To make every movement a thing of grace and beauty," she says. "That is my one and only desire." The camel does not stop practicing even when her feet become blistered and her body aches with fatigue. At last she announces, "Now I am a dancer." But when she dances before invited friends and critics they do *not* applaud. In fact, they are dismissive and cruel in their candid assessment of her abilities. "I must tell you frankly," said a member of the audience, "as a critic and a spokesman for this group, that you are lumpy and humpy. You are baggy and bumpy. You are, like the rest of us, simply a camel. You are *not* and never will be a ballet dancer!" But she is not convinced. She reasons that since she has worked so hard she must be a splendid dancer. She continued to dance (for herself), and this brought her great pleasure. According to Lobel, the moral of this fable is that "satisfaction will come to those who please themselves."[1]

Both the story and the moral are charmingly ambiguous. Should we aim to *only* please ourselves? When are we each the best judges of our own aspirations and activities? To whom should we listen when critical advice is offered? The plausibility of this fable moral depends on a variety of circumstances that are worth exploring, not just about camels who love to dance, but also about the circumstances connected to our own passions, ambitions, and commitment to these projects. Importantly, the camel's story tells us something about hobbies in general, that these are activities shaped by an amateur's particular love for the activity and that they are marked by a devotion to trying to improve. But what remains elusive is the stamp of excellence for both the camel and for the rest of us who mimic her dedication to "make every movement a thing of grace and beauty" by practicing over and over our respective pirouettes, relevés, and arabesques. Are we all merely recreational athletes who cannot possibly aim for excellence because we have virtually no hope of winning a competition? Are we like the ice-skater who demands an "A for effort" even though we cannot even get off the ice to perform a triple jump? The camel continues to dance *for herself*, and Lobel seems to imply that this is a satisfying outcome. But I think we can say more about how excellence finds its natural home in the practice of a hobby.

Recreation

For the past 50 years my practice of recreational activities includes the following: dog obedience, horses, swimming, running, biking, skiing, tennis, golfing, kayaking, playing the flute, and dog agility. Since I was 10 years old I've been devoted to a variety of sports with varying degrees of commitment, for fluctuating periods of time. There are some activities in which I have always wanted to excel; being an Olympic rider was my heart's desire when I was young. This aspiration inspired me while playing with Breyer horse models, when I was on my hands and knees pretending to be a horse, or practicing running the Kentucky Derby against my best friend, Linda, every day at recess in elementary school. When I finally actually owned a horse, I was ecstatic. The most mundane details consumed all of my attention and time. I would daydream through the school day in anticipation of going to the stable to ride and count down the days

Canine Agility and the Meaning of Excellence

until my Friday riding lesson on my own horse. I remember a week spent at Girl Scout camp, so completely homesick that I cried the whole time: on hikes, while making crafts, at meals, and at night on my cot. The only times I would pause in my crying jags were those moments when I remembered that I had a Friday afternoon riding lesson. I imagined that if I could only get through the week to my scheduled lesson, everything would be okay.

Horses went on hold for a good part of my adult life while I went to college and to graduate school, applied for jobs, got married, and started a family. But my horse-love craziness was merely lurking in the background, waiting to bubble up and take over my life again. Riding horses as an adult is a completely different thing. It turned out that I was more ambitious as an adult. I chased an ideal, hoping to buy and train a young athletic horse for eventing, one that I could compete and one that would allow me to develop my dressage and jumping skills. Of course, readers will know how this usually goes, like a snowball picking up snow on a downhill slope. The horse needed training. I needed lessons. We needed to travel to competitions and to prepare for these. Time, time, time, money, money, money. Why did I do it? Because I have always deeply loved horses, their beautiful, graceful bodies, the look of a horse jumping with front feet tucked up around the chin and the back rounded, the sensation of a horse's soft mouth in my hands, and his rocking horse canter pushing me out of the saddle slightly. Decades later I can put myself to sleep by remembering my horse's floating trot, even and regular with his body slightly bent to the inside in a corner of the arena, his head on the vertical, while I take a light feel of his mouth. He is relaxed and sensitive in my hands as they close slightly and then open, to communicate a bend here, a little collection there. And finally I feel my horse coming up underneath me with a round frame that feels like we are both in balance. The trot is springy, floaty, forward, and soft.

When I reflect about my recreational activities over the years, I discern different motivational states. Running, biking, cross-country skiing, and swimming I do for fitness, although I do love to be in the water. Kayaking I do for pleasure but I've recently recognized how ideal it is for building upper body strength. Tennis,

Four. Agility as Hobby

golf and playing the flute are so, so hard. There are moments of thrilling success but these are overshadowed by feeling like such a poor athlete or musician that it is difficult to take a great deal of satisfaction in these activities. There are two points I want to make. First, I am ridiculously attached to improvement and to the development of skill, irrespective of the activity I undertake. This does not mean that I *actually* improve. Sometimes getting better is noticeable (to me) however negligible it seems in the overall scheme of things. Later in this chapter we will want to say more about what it means to "try to get better." For now I will merely list the ingredients: practice, lessons, practice, reading, practice, thinking, practice, imaging, practice. Second, there is one kind of activity that continues to qualify as a passion: training animals, specifically dogs and horses. The competition part flows naturally from training but I watched my zeal for competing horses gradually peter out altogether. I am still on the fence about agility competitions. Let me explain why.

You may remember from an earlier chapter that Maggie suffered a bout of lameness. It was a good nine weeks before it was diagnosed as a lingering inflammation of the tendon in her left wrist. The rehabilitation back to agility for a tendon injury needs to be slow and gradual. This I learned as the weeks passed and I was still leash-walking Maggie, trudging up and down hills, standing her on three legs, walking her backwards, and sideways up and down hills, asking her to sit and then stand up and down hills, etc. If you have ever done anything like this with your dog, then you know that it is a painfully measured process. All of my plans to compete at this or that trial ground to a halt. Meanwhile, most of my agility friends were attending workshops, classes, and trials. It astounds me how easily a person can drop out of sight in the agility community. All you have to do is to stop showing up.

As I write this chapter Maggie is on weeks three and four of rehabilitation after her initial diagnosis. She is allowed to run a short, straight tunnel for five repetitions every other day. This may not seem like much but I am thoroughly excited. The point of all this is not to elicit sympathy from the reader. It is to document my own psychological recovery. When it began to sink in that my

Canine Agility and the Meaning of Excellence

agility activity was on hold for an indefinite period of time, I was so lost. Initially, I wasn't even sure that Maggie would come back to sport fitness. Training routines and my social network of agility friends dropped completely and suddenly out of my life. Moreover, it felt like nothing really could take its place. Merely substituting another activity for agility, like running or swimming, was absurd. Just impossible.

But the surprising thing I learned about this three-month hiatus from agility is that I was not willing to give it up so easily. All of the other recreational activities that I have undertaken in my life have not had the same claim on me. Swimming, tennis, running, and even playing the flute are activities that come and go. I am not bereft when my attention turns elsewhere. Horses just got too expensive. My ex-husband called my riding a "black hole for money." He was right about that. But my love for agility is not so easy to relinquish. Because Maggie was rehabbing, I started to train my husband's two-year-old birddog, Lukas, in a foundation agility class. Next I returned to my advanced agility class, without a dog, to practice walking and running courses and sequences. I didn't want my handling skills to atrophy (such as they were). And I missed my instructor and classmates. I am not special in these respects. Many other practitioners of this sport would do the same thing. But what I would like to emphasize is that for me agility is a love affair. It hits a particular sweet spot that includes training animals, the company of my dog, Maggie, competition, reflection and problem solving, the social network of agility friends, and just trying to get better, inch by inch. Many weeks of rehabilitating Maggie reminded me that the competition part of my appetite for agility is just a small piece. I am ecstatic to have her back in the practice ring, even if we run 10 repetitions of a straight line of jumps set at 12 inches.

Perhaps readers have the same kind of love affair with agility; maybe that's why you bought (or borrowed) this book in the first place. But if it is something else to which you are seriously devoted, then you will still know what I mean. The problem with calling these love affairs "hobbies" is that the connotation is misleading. Like Maggie, the concept of a hobby also wants rehabilitation.

Four. Agility as Hobby

"The Gentle Pursuit of a Modest Competence"

The dancing camel is a good place to start. One way of viewing her dancing aspiration is to imagine that she is struggling to achieve excellence. If so, then according to Tim Wu (2018), the camel assumes without reflection that her dancing hobby must be a display of skill and that she must be exceptional at what she does.

> If you're a jogger, it is no longer enough to cruise around the block; you're training for the next marathon. If you're a painter, you are no longer passing a pleasant afternoon, just you, your watercolors and your water lilies; you are trying to land a gallery show or at least garner a respectable social media following.... Lost here is *the gentle pursuit of a modest competence* [my emphasis], the doing of something just because you enjoy it, not because you are good at it. Hobbies, let me remind you, are supposed to be something different from work. But alien values like "the pursuit of excellence" have crept into and corrupted what was once the realm of leisure, leaving little room for the true amateur.

In other words, it is the amateur's misguided pursuit of excellence that has corrupted the realm of leisure. Wu is not disparaging those among us who are pursuing agility, dancing, or other sports at the highest level of mastery. But he invites us to consider the contrasting experience, one which he describes as "a real and pure joy, a sweet, childlike delight that comes from just learning and trying to get better." The heartbreak for most of us who undertake the sport of agility (or dance) is that expecting, hoping, and struggling for excellence can be an impediment. In Chapter One we testified to the psychological disvalue of striving for exceptional performance and invariably falling short. According to Wu, demanding excellence in our hobbies "steals from us one of life's greatest rewards—the simple pleasure of doing something you merely, but truly, enjoy."

When we learn that the camel continues to dance in spite of the critics' cruel assessment of her skill, we see that she exhibits a quality familiar to other amateur athletes: the discipline of practice and effort that continues to inspire and to drive us forward in our activities. The camel's dancing is an activity that she genuinely and truly enjoys. By continuing to dance with commitment and love, she engages in the "gentle pursuit of a modest competence." But what does this mean, exactly, for those of us who participate in agility as a hobby?

What Is a Hobby?

In *A Sand County Almanac*, Aldo Leopold (1966, 181) ventures this description of a hobby:

> I cannot easily imagine a greater fallacy than for one who has several hobbies to speak on the subject to those who may have none.... You do not annex a hobby, the hobby annexes you. To prescribe a hobby would be dangerously akin to prescribing a wife—with about the same probability of a happy outcome.

Leopold laments his inability to mark the difference between hobbies and normal pursuits, but he does submit that they need no rational justification. To offer a justification for a hobby is to incorrectly describe it as an "exercise undertaken for health, power, or profit." Making a longbow is one example of a hobby, as is falconry. If a person can make something, or make the tools to make it with, "and then use it to accomplish some needless thing," then that person is engaged in the kind of activity Leopold would call a hobby. Further, a hobby is "a defiance of the contemporary." It is a gamble, and it may be "a solitary revolt against the common-place" (Leopold 1966, 187). Leopold is inviting us to elevate the role of leisure in our lives and stressing the importance of engaging in a pursuit that requires no rationalization.[2] Hobbies defy the "commonplace" expectation to engage always in work. Hobbies are a relief from work. But on the classical account of leisure, we should not merely think of hobbies as time off or simply recovery from work. Leisure is *activity*, not merely rest. Think about the time, money, and attention we exert on behalf of agility training and competition. Even if we try to explain or justify this "expense," we will probably not convince anyone but the members of our own agility community. As Leopold would say, it is "the joint conspiracy of a congenial group."

Four. Agility as Hobby

Characterizing agility as a hobby might seem like a concession for most of us. Perhaps by doing so we believe that we have given up something crucial or essential in the practice of our sport, the competitive ideal. So if we participate in the sport of agility as a hobby, what does this really mean? To begin, *who* are sport hobbyists?

> Its players set no records, receive no headlines, and rarely worry about winning any championships. They vary in age from youngsters still learning their game to senior citizens hoping to maintain their skills or slow their rate of decline. Yet, all of them have one thing in common … a hard-to-explain love affair with a game, a relationship that brightens their lives in measurable ways. These individuals are typically members of subcultures of runners, bikers, golfers, and others who, with only moderate degrees of success, playfully and seriously tilt with their own sporting windmills. For every low handicap golfer or sub-3-h marathoner, one can find many hundreds of committed hackers and weekend runners who will never approach even the most liberal standards of performative excellence [Kretchmar 2019, 368].

"These are my people," I say to myself. Yet there is still a moment of hesitation that maybe others feel as well. How can my practice of agility be *merely* a hobby? This characterization fails to capture how serious I am about this sport: thinking about courses and sequences, thinking about how to train my dog, taking lessons and seminars and, yes, still entering competitive trials. Perhaps this reticence to characterize our practice of agility as a hobby is the result of some preconceived ideas about the concept of a hobby, that hobbyists putter about with no real commitment to their activities. Consider this alternative proposed by Kretchmar (2019, 375), who suggests that "intensity of meaning, purposeful caring and ardent striving" typify the sport hobbyist.

> Hobbies are not necessarily domains for dabbling or trifling. But neither are they places that require their inhabitants to grind their way to excellence. Hobbies are activities to which we return repeatedly because we like to be in their company. We look forward to seeing them again and again. In this sense, they are, or at least can be, like old friends. As life-long associates, hobbies adorn our lives, providing meaningful company and identity, two factors that can be overlooked in cultures focused on achievement and excellence.

Canine Agility and the Meaning of Excellence

In addition to the central role that agility plays in our lives, hobbies also capture our aspirations to do better and to improve. But, importantly, our aspirations to improve are shared by all of us who practice the sport. This means that elite performers have something in common with those who are only moderately competent. Both aim at progress. Elite performers aim for perfection; those who are moderately competent may aim to just get it right (Kretchmar 2019, 378).

This way of thinking about agility-as-hobby suggests a tentative answer to the question "Why am I doing this?" Practicing a start-line stay, asking for a long send to a tunnel, or a surge ahead "go" line at the end of a course are all occasions for me to "aim at progress." These might be in competitive settings at a trial or sequences I practice at home. In these cases I formulate a specific aspiration that is relative to me, my dog, and the context in which I participate in agility. No doubt the result will not be perfection, but it may capture a passion that I have for just trying to get it right. As Kretchmar (2019, 378) suggests, this aspiration puts me "on a level normative playing field with those with more impressive endowments, aspirations, and accomplishments."

Consider another characteristic of hobbies. The kinds of experiences we accrue when we participate in a hobby include gaining and refining skills, visioning goals, and maybe revising these in light of successes and failures. This is a *storyline* that emerges from a particular person, their history and capabilities, and their interests. For example, when I was first introduced to the sport of agility and began to attend classes and practice sessions, I did not have a competitive goal. I just liked the idea of training my dog and spending time with her. Then my objectives gradually changed as we learned more. Now I focus on course strategy, learning when to run ahead or to wait patiently for a turn, how to position my feet, hands, and shoulders, and how to manage an over-aroused dog. Each person who undertakes this sport has his or her own story—from early introductions to agility, transitioning to growth, sometimes accompanied by frustrations and disappointment and, ideally, onto new projects and goals (Kretchmar 2019, 379). But the *value* of these experiences does not depend on exceptional performance and rarefied results. Rather, it lies in "the quality of relationships between oneself and the world" (Dewey [1934] 2005, 42).

The Amateur Hour

Consider one case study of an amateur. Meet C. Wayne Booth, amateur cello player. In his memoir, *For the Love of It: Amateuring and Its Rivals*, Booth (1999) describes his longstanding devotion to learning to play the cello at a rather late stage in life. He admits to being not very good. But he is also capable of brilliant moments, after practicing and practicing. These flashes of virtuosity emerge in lovely collaboration with other musicians playing chamber music. What distinguishes the amateur from the professional? According to Booth (1999, 6–7) amateurs are seeking accomplishment but the purpose of the pursuit is puzzling since success is "always out of sight."

> Why go on taking lessons and practicing daily when every playing session demonstrates that you will always play worse than every cellist, even the worst, in the youth orchestra you heard last week.... Why attempt the impossible?

The obvious answer to the question "Why attempt the impossible?" is that it leads to a certain kind of pleasure or satisfaction. But Booth insists that when the amateur practices a hobby, she is not merely seeking what he calls "ice-cream pleasures." The amateur is laboring, learning to do it better. The practice of the activity "lands us in aspirations that can produce a sense of failure." Recall how some people who "play" agility with their dogs do so without regard to trying to get better. They may be engaged in a certain kind of play that is rewarding for both handler and dog. But perhaps the kind of pleasure that may bring is what Booth means by "ice-cream pleasure."

> Even when amateuring does not produce minor disasters, it always reveals this one major difference from all the other kinds of loving play: the amateur *works* at it, or at least has done so in the past, aspiring to some level of competence or mastery or know-how or expertise. The

amateur wants more of it not just because more brings more pleasure. More ice-cream will *almost* always give me more pleasure, but loving to gorge on ice-cream does not make me an amateur; working hard to earn money to buy more ice-cream or a bigger yacht does not entitle the lover to membership in our unsecret society [Booth 1999, 12].

A necessary condition about amateuring is that you try to get better all the time. Booth calls this the "daily betterment command." Amateurs invest action in their hobbies by acquiring experiences, judgment and discrimination, and by paying attention. "The thrill seeker becomes an amateur only when he chooses to *practice* something like hang gliding ..." (Booth 1999, 57).

The Core of Excellence

Many people will say that only professionals can be excellent. Kretchmar and Wu maintain that when the hobbyist believes that they must "grind their way to excellence," then this idea might actually interfere with doing something just for the enjoyment it brings to the hobbyist. So does it even make sense to say that an amateur cello player, a tennis player, or a practitioner of agility can be excellent? My answer is yes but we will have to relinquish a few prejudices about the concept of excellence itself, while retaining a core concept that most of us will recognize. I would like to suggest that the concept of excellence need not be defined in such a way as to require exceptional performance. Instead there are a number of features of excellence that typify this concept for all practitioners of the sport including highly experienced handlers and their elite dogs as well as amateur handlers who are merely competent. One strategy for identifying a core concept of excellence is to try to say what amateurs and professionals have in common. Booth (1999, 16) describes this point of intersection for musicians in the following way:

- Both are making music, not just listening;
- both are playing the same music; and
- both are displaying a keenness to excel, with or without reward.

Four. Agility as Hobby

Of course, there is no mistaking the difference between these two kinds of musicians. It is not merely that the professional gets paid to perform; that feature seems incidental to the distinction. Rather, it is that the professional produces a performance that is typically awe-inspiring. It is an *exceptional performance*. That's why we pay money to go to a concert performed by professionals, buy a CD of a well-known orchestra, or subscribe to a classical music website that profiles virtuoso performances. But why does the concept of excellence require exceptional performance? This is a question about the concept of excellence itself. I recommend that we follow Booth's description of what amateur and professional musicians have in common. So the core concept of excellence in agility includes

- practicing or competing in the sport of agility (vs. watching these activities);
- following the same rules of the sport of agility; and
- displaying an eagerness to practice the activity of agility with skill and to seek to improve these skills.

Many displays of excellence will indeed be cases of exceptional performance. But if an agility team displays a competent performance and also satisfies these three conditions, then this may be considered excellent also. This is possible because we have rehabilitated the concept of a hobby. Hobbies are undertaken by those who are engaged in a serious love affair with an activity. Amateurs are not "dabbling" or merely engaging in "primitive play" like a baby who delights in splashing her bathwater. Those who undertake "serious leisure" are committed to improving their skills and striving to get better. For this population excellence applies to those who display exceptional performance as well as to those amateurs whose performances might be considered merely competent.

An Objection

One standard objection to this position is that by crediting the amateur agility team with excellence, we have "inflated" the concept of excellence. Kretchmar (2019, 373) remarks that if we relax the standards for achieving excellence then we risk the "potential loss of discriminating benchmarks for excellence.... Increased access [to excellence], in other words, rescues the intelligibility of questing for more athletes but commensurately diminishes the worth of their achievement." So the basic worry is that if the mere amateur who practices a hobby can be excellent regardless of the performance itself, then anyone can be excellent. And if anyone can be excellent, then excellence has lost its rarified value in general. But it does not follow that if amateurs who practice a hobby can be excellent, then anyone can be excellent. This is because undertaking a hobby is an activity that is more robust as we have described.

For example, the dancing camel seems to satisfy the three conditions for being an amateur who dances. She engages in the activity rather than just watching others dance. She practices the very same ballet movements that a professional dancer practices. And she is devoted to improving her skills by practicing these movements every day "under the hot desert sun." But according to the critics who watch her recital, the performance itself leaves something to be desired. It is not exceptional. Is the camel an *excellent* dancer? Those who believe that excellence requires exceptional performance would say no. But I disagree. By calling her dancing excellent we have not cheapened the value of excellence. The camel does not just get an "A for effort." She is not excellent merely because she is trying hard or exhibiting a strong work ethic. Rather, she undertakes an activity with the same level of seriousness as the professional dancer. She knows enough about the basic positions of dance in order to practice *these* positions rather than some random movements. She knows enough about what skills are required for ballet in order to try to improve these particular skills. The camel's storyline is not readily apparent in this short fable. If we had a more complete account we might learn how she came to love this activity in the first place and why she pursues it so ardently. We might learn also how disappointments led her to form new goals and aspirations. Maybe her choice to dance in order to please only herself was born out of the disparaging critics who attended her recital. In other words, the objection articulated above, that we have inflated the concept of excellence, fails to get its grip on the amateur hobbyist, whether it is the dancing

Four. Agility as Hobby

camel or a beginning student of agility and her novice dog. This is so because we are not merely contrasting competent performance with exceptional performance. Instead we are telling a story about a person who undertakes an activity out of love and labors in the company of this activity, acquiring knowledge, skills, and greater expertise. This is what we have learned from rehabilitating the concept of a hobby.

How do we know who deserves to be called excellent in agility if we do not use the display of exceptional performance as a measure of excellence? In my opinion, the elements of excellence emerge from a particular story about a particular person and her performance dog. This storyline captures an individual's history, capabilities, interests, and intentions about future projects and goals. The stories we seek about excellence displayed by agility handlers and their dogs are those that capture the "meaningful directions" of the hobbyist and "a coherent storyline" (Kretchmar 2019, 379). Ideally, we need to know also what the handler is *trying to do* in the practice ring or in the competitive trial setting. Consider my own story.

Maggie is an over-aroused dog; she is almost jumping out of her skin at a trial. So what I often try to do in that context is less. I might only train the start line. Sometimes I will train just the bottom of the A-frame and release her to the next jump if she stays in position. When these small moments work, it does feel spectacular. This is not based on any exceptional performance per se. I haven't earned a qualifying run. In many cases I haven't even completed the course. Rather, it is an exercise performed proficiently that we both need in order to bring the energy level down a notch for both of us. But given my history with this dog, my relative inexperience, and my modest aims in the ring, we are, for a moment, excellent.

These kinds of stories exemplify more than "trying hard." They situate the handler and the dog in a training relation and in circumstances that display the handler's informed, situated knowledge and problem-solving. Notice that we cannot say the same about Dusty and Rob (see Chapter One). Although Rob wants desperately to succeed, the kind of success he wants is a particular outcome: winning at agility competitions. The strange quality of Rob's story for genuine lovers of agility is how little we learn about Dusty's preparation, including the details of practice sessions. Nowhere do we see the *training* of Rob and Dusty and a devotion to the acquisition of skills needed in order to compete successfully. In this case, the context necessary for assessing excellence is just unavailable to the reader. Just because Dusty often fails to qualify in a competitive trial setting does not mean that he fails to display excellence. Besides beating the other competitors, what is Rob trying to do?

Does Your Dog Have a Hobby?

Characterizing agility as a hobby undertaken by amateurs sounds plausible to most practitioners of the sport. But without a doubt this analysis is incomplete since agility is not just about the handler. Does your dog have a hobby? If so, is that hobby merely an extension of your hobby? What we have learned about human hobbies is that they are voluntarily chosen with intentional seriousness, much like a labor of love. Humans who undertake particular activities as hobbies seek to improve their skill and expertise. As well these activities are practiced for rewards that are more like internal satisfactions. The activities are done for their own sake. So can any of these repeated voluntary actions and intentions be sensibly attributed to an agility dog? A good place to start is to read Lund's (2014, 110–11) description of the agility dog's "canine agency and authority."

> The agility arena becomes a testing ground for this ability to read and respond to the canine. It encourages the attempt to understand and communicate with the other, yet it also vividly reminds people of the limits of their comprehension and control, as they find themselves, for that moment in the ring, at the mercy of the dog.... Compliance is not at issue so much as interpretation, discrimination, and judgment.

The language used here is crucial to reading the agility team as a human-canine partnership that is shaped by how the dog feels: joyful, frustrated, confused, or uncertain. Moreover, the autonomy of the dog is captured by crediting her with complex choices that involve "interpretation, discrimination, and judgment." However, even if we credit the agility dog with the "authority of judgment" in the moments when she is running a course with her handler, is this the same thing as voluntarily choosing to take part in the activity of agility in general? What would count as evidence that an agility dog is seeking to improve her skills and expertise? And what exactly is the dog's reward for this activity? These are all questions that invite us to take up the point of view of the agility dog herself. Those who are best positioned to answer these questions are the owners of dogs who practice agility, so I asked a few agility handlers: Does your dog have a hobby? This is what they had to say.

JoLee Yeddo: Tyrion's hobby is anything that is fun and active. So if I'm doing something in the house, he'll bring me a toy to tug with. And if that's not the right one, he'll bring another toy to tug with, and then he'll let go of it. And he wants me to throw it or tug it or something. And then if that's not going to work, he'll get a bone and he'll chew the bone. And then if it looks like I might do something, he'll come and bring me something. He wants to interact. He wants to play. A hobby is something we choose to do all the time, right? Arya's hobby really is napping in her crate away from everything, like shutting out the world. She really likes to do that. Wembley, if he could, would eat all the dirt in the yard. He likes to get a dirt clod and shake all the dirt off of it and then eat it. It's fun for him. He rather enjoys that.

Jodi Pangman: There are millions of dogs in households that do nothing. They are just pets, and they are perfectly happy with that. They don't have any hobbies. They don't crochet or anything. They could have a hobby killing squirrels out in the yard. I mean, I don't know.

Well, the consensus is still out on dogs and hobbies. Let me know what you think.

Introducing Ann Benjamin and Jodi Pangman

Ann: I'm Ann Benjamin. I have two Aussies and I run a Boston Terrier part-time. My oldest Aussie is 10 years old. He's retired from all but A.K.C. agility. I mean, that's about it. They primarily do agility. I'll let Jodi cover what else the older Aussie does.

Canine Agility and the Meaning of Excellence

Jodi Pangman runs Whimsy through an A.K.C. Jumpers course. Southern Adirondack Agility Club, High Goal Farm, August 2023 (photograph by David K. Cerilli).

Jodi: I'm Jodi Pangman. I run a Boston Terrier part-time, an Aussie part-time. My oldest is retired. She's 10 years old, so she's retired completely from agility. She does scent work now, and so does the oldest. And I do scent work with the oldest Aussie, Dobby. I also have a six-year-old Toy Fox Terrier, Demi. She only does agility part-time because she has some motivation problems. And I've just started doing Fast Cat with the Toy Fox Terrier just for something else to do with her.

So when and why did you begin to do agility with your dogs?

Ann: Well, it's been over 20 years for me. My first dog was an American Eskimo. I was doing obedience as a member of a dog club. I saw them doing agility outside on the agility course, and I asked my obedience instructor if she thought my dog could do it. She said, "I think she'll be great at it." I just wanted to do something with my dog to get us both out of the house. I never anticipated competing. But I trained her for two years and then got talked into going to a

Four. Agility as Hobby

competition trial. She was fabulous. I was hooked, and that's why I've been doing it for 20 years.

Jodi: As a kid, I loved purebred dogs. And I was interested in the confirmation aspect of it. But I had a little mixed-breed that I taught tricks and stuff to when I was a kid. So as an adult, I never thought I would ever be able to afford a purebred dog. I had a mixed breed that was just a pet. I didn't do anything with her. And then in 1994–1995 I found a dog who turned out to be an American Eskimo. I put up flyers. Somebody's got to own her. Nobody ever stepped forward to claim her. She was smart as a whip, but she was fearful. I decided, "Well, let me put her into some obedience classes and get her a little better socialized." No one had even heard of agility then. And I wasn't good at it. I couldn't do front crosses. I didn't know how to read my dog. She was very driven and would zoom around the ring. I couldn't understand what to do. I would try to drive her from the rear. But when she was ahead of me she didn't handle that well. But I didn't know how to do anything differently. I used to watch how people walked the course and then walk it the same way and try to run her that way, and she didn't like it at all. She was 12 years old when she got her Excellent A.K.C. titles and then she retired promptly from that. She loved it. She loved it. She thought it was great. But she was a clown. Often, if she saw somebody that she knew, she would run out of the ring to go see them. I just had no clue, and I didn't enjoy it. It wasn't a lot of fun for me. But I had an attitude. I'm not going to let this sport get the better of me. I went to a Vizla from the Eskimo. He was more of a disaster. Yeah, because he was very high-drive. If I had him now it would be different. But he taught me a ton. In my first few dogs, I didn't have a lot of success like Ann did. We often failed. It was awful.

What does excellence look like in the practice ring or in competition?
Jodi: I think every person and dog's journey is different. What's excellence to one person is different to the next person. I have multiple championships, but I've never had any desire to be on a world team. I just want to do my own personal best. I set my own personal goals and then I try to accomplish them. My thing has always been doing something with a breed that's not a breed you look at and say,

Canine Agility and the Meaning of Excellence

"Oh, they're agility dogs." That's the mark I want to make. I just think it's all about the bond you have with your dog and how close you get to your dog. Every journey and every agility trip you take with a different dog is different, and they all teach you something new.

Ann: Well, just this past Friday, we had a private lesson to try to get our dogs to do more distance from us. We were given some distance challenges to try, but we weren't successful right away. Then all of a sudden it made sense to both of us. That's excellence to me. We both understood and then we did the exercise successfully. I thought I would handle it one way, but our instructor said, "No, try this." I thought, "That's never going work." Then my dog just went out so easily. For us it was a case of training excellence because both of us learned something.

Is excellence in agility the same as earning a qualifying run?

Jodi: I learned moments. You're going to string more of those moments together. You're going to get to that qualifying run eventually if you have faith. That's the only thing that really kept me in the game. We failed more than we were successful. My classmates and I started as equals, but then they soared past me in the competitions. Yeah. It's moments for me.

Do you think that a novice dog and handler can be excellent?

Jodi: Absolutely. Yeah. Absolutely. Oh, my God. Yes. You see it. You see the brilliance. You'll see a dog and they'll start off rough. The dog is zooming all over the place. And then in the middle of the course, they'll pull it together. They just pull it together. And the middle through the end is flawless. The handler comes off and they are so disappointed that they didn't qualify. "But didn't you see what happened in the middle? In the end, you were completely connected. You were flawless." That's a glimpse of what's going to happen.

Ann: We try to notice that when we are watching the newer people who are first competing. And we tell them that they earned a "personal Q." That means that you didn't necessarily qualify according to the rules of the game, but you got a personal Q because your dog entered the weave poles on the first time, or your dog did the See-Saw with confidence, or your dog held his start line on that day, or whatever.

Four. Agility as Hobby

Jodi: It's interesting that you have to remind novice handlers with novice dogs about that. They're disappointed because they didn't qualify, but they have to be redirected about how they think about what they're doing. Try to see what went well in your run. What went well? What were you most proud of in your run that you and your dog did? And that can be excellent.

Summary

So what have we learned about hobbies? From Leopold we understand how hobbies are undertaken as leisure activities. Leisure does not merely mean rest or recovery from work. Rather, these are *active* loves that are chosen for their own sake. Kretchmar and Wu remind us that these activities have the potential to brighten our lives, even if our skill and performance is merely competent, not exceptional. In fact, we may lose sight of the simple enjoyment

Ann Benjamin has a good connection with her dog, Shout. Port Chester Obedience Training Club A.K.C. Trial at Dream Dogs Training Center, Saugerties, New York, November 2023 (artsyfartsyphotosbyshanon.com).

Canine Agility and the Meaning of Excellence

of hobbies if we are driven to excel or believe that we must "grind our way to excellence." Hobbies shape our identities and they collect like-minded practitioners that form a community. Most important, amateur hobbyists do indeed have aspirations to improve their skills. They do not dabble. Rather, they try to get better. The storyline of the amateur is marked by one's motivations to undertake a hobby in the first place, gaining and refining skills relevant to that activity, visioning goals, and experiencing successes as well as failures and disappointments, leading to new projects and goals. This very individual story unfolds over time. It captures the rich texture and quality of the relation between oneself and the world. The hobbyist and the professional have something in common, and that is the aspiration to improve their skills and to acquire expertise. The professional may aim for perfection while the amateur may aim for just getting it right on occasion. Each kind of realized ambition may be a display of excellence.

I want to return once more to the dancing camel. One question we might ask about Lobel's fable is whether or not the camel, or anyone else, should take the critic's remarks seriously. Recall that a "spokesman" charges the camel with being "lumpy and humpy." She is simply a camel, and the critic declares that she is not now a ballet dancer nor will she ever be one. So who is the critic? What does this reviewer know about the standards of excellent dancing? This is actually a significant question, not just about a camel who undertakes ballet as serious hobby, but for all amateurs who tenaciously seek to develop skills, expertise, and knowledge about their respective hobbies. Whether I approximate or fall short of a standard of excellence in agility is not just determined by me. But if I am not the sole judge, then who determines these standards? And how do I become confidently familiar with them? To answer these questions we turn next to MacIntyre's (1981) account of a *practice* and to the internal goods associated with the practice of agility, in particular.

FIVE

The Internal Goods of Agility

> *A practice involves standards of excellence and obedience to rules as well as the achievement of goods. To enter into a practice is to accept the authority of those standards and the inadequacy of my own performance as judged by them* (MacIntyre 1984, 190).

At the end of the last chapter we asked a fundamental question about Lobel's charming fable, "The Camel Dances." We wanted to know whether or not the critic had any authority, knowledge, or expertise about ballet dancing in order to justify the comment that the camel is "not and never will be a dancer." The question begs to be answered for those of us amateurs who resolutely pursue a difficult hobby like agility. In fact, we might articulate one of the main questions of this book by asking, "Who displays excellence in agility, and how do we know it?" Although the camel continues to dance "in order to please herself," this does not mean that she is an excellent dancer. And, similarly, even if we agility practitioners continue to participate in this sport for the pleasures that it produces, this will not necessarily mean that we are each displaying excellence. In this chapter I will argue that the best way to understand who displays excellence in agility is to situate this activity in a larger social and historical context where the standards of excellence are specific to this activity and determined by the esteemed practitioners who participate in it. This recommendation about how to understand excellence is characteristic of what philosopher Alasdair MacIntyre (1984) calls a "practice" in his renowned book *After Virtue*. I will take some liberties with this concept as it is originally described by MacIntyre. In my opinion, developing a *neo–MacIntyrean* account of a practice is the best way to profile the idea that agility is not merely a human activity but is fundamentally about the distinctive relationship between a human handler and a dog.

Internal and External Rewards

Suppose I entice a new agility handler and her novice dog into the sport by promising to pay her a significant amount of money for practicing agility twice a week and running courses cleanly (or with few faults) in agility class or at a competitive trial. Who is this imaginary person? Let's assume that this new handler is named Babs, 65 years old, physically active, retired, and living on a smallish fixed income. Her dog is in good health, fairly obedient, and willing to try new activities. In other words, the handler has the time to do agility and a companion dog teammate but few resources to avidly pursue the sport. If she acquires the skills and learns the rules and practices, she may well produce clean runs in agility class or qualifying runs at competitive agility trials. As promised, this will ensure that Babs is able to supplement her modest income and live rather comfortably. If she is *solely* motivated to receive the money, then her handling skills may be less than perfect. In fact, they may be deplorable if her cues are unclear to the dog, inefficient, and disorganized. But whatever works to produce a clean run will be good enough to receive the monetary reward.[1]

Why do we need to imagine such a person? Isn't she an *atypical* agility practitioner? Yes, I believe Babs is rather different than most of us who do agility. But hypothetical Babs allows us to mark a significant distinction. Because Babs is motivated by the money she receives for the outcome of her activity, she is thereby motivated by an *external reward* or "good." Another way of putting this is to say that money is external to the activity of agility itself since she might undertake alternative activities for the same kind of reward. For example, she might acquire money by hustling pool in a local bar.

The contrasting motivation is more difficult to specify. Following MacIntyre we will call these "internal rewards" or goods.

Five. The Internal Goods of Agility

Consider a slightly different scenario. Even though Babs is initially motivated by the money, her handling skills gradually improve and she pays more attention to the physical and mental challenges of the sport, especially in regard to her dog. She finds herself puzzling about how to perform a blind cross in a timely manner on a course, and she now understands how crucial it is to stay connected with her dog. Pretty soon she (mostly) forgets about the money. Instead she enrolls in a seminar with a well-known trainer and begins to practice in her own backyard, turning this way and that, running straight ahead with her head tilted sideways, looking over her shoulder either left or right. These skills that she seeks to improve include mental preparation such as imagining where her dog will be on a course and where she needs to be in order to ensure the next obstacle is cued correctly. She also aspires to improve her physical skills, running fast ahead of her dog and also decelerating in other places to prepare her dog for a turn. There is a lot to think about and remember. But as she improves she gains a kind of internal satisfaction about what she can do together with her partner dog. In other words, over time Babs participates in the activity of agility for the sake of internal rewards or goods. These rewards are specific to the activity of agility itself. They may include handling skills, course strategy, working as a team with her dog, and mental acuity while in motion on a practice course or in a competitive setting. These goods cannot be acquired by any other means unless the activity is relevantly like agility. Moreover, even though imaginary Babs makes the transition from external rewards to internal rewards of the sport, this transition is not inevitable for any of us who practice agility. MacIntyre (1984, 188) says this about the intelligent child who initially learns to play chess in order to receive candy:

> But, *so we may hope* [my emphasis], there will come a time when the child will find in those goods specific to chess, in the achievement of a certain highly particular kind of analytical skill, strategic imagination and competitive intensity, a new set of reasons, reasons now not just for winning on a particular occasion, but for trying to excel in whatever way the game of chess demands. Now if the child cheats, he or she will be defeating not me, but himself or herself.

Canine Agility and the Meaning of Excellence

The relevance of our hypothetical novice handler, Babs, is now coming into sharper focus. By profiling the internal rewards of an activity we are closer to identifying what makes for excellence relative to that activity. Trying to excel in "whatever way the game of [agility] demands" means to pursue the internal goods of agility. These internal goods include, for example, *trying to improve mental and physical handling skills, envisioning practical course strategies, working together as a human-dog team, and cultivating mental alertness while in motion on an agility course*. If Babs is motivated to pursue the internal goods of agility, then, in a sense, she is enamored with the sport itself and all that is required in order to improve her skills and expertise. This allows us to say why the amateur hobbyist steadfastly pursues an activity like music, dance, or agility, despite the fact that her performance may fall considerably short of exceptional. As we have already said, this does not mean that the amateur is merely seeking a pleasurable experience, what Booth calls "ice-cream pleasures." Laboring to improve one's skills is not necessarily or always pleasurable. However, the amateur agility practitioner, like our imaginary Babs, may derive satisfaction from gaining expertise and knowledge. Now we have a vocabulary and a particular way of describing what the novice handler and the seasoned agility practitioner have in common. They are both primarily motivated to pursue the internal rewards of the sport. This kind of motivation can be distinguished from the external reasons for undertaking an activity like agility. These can be described as participating in the sport because one *solely* wants to acquire ribbons, titles, championships, or acquire recognition, or attain status. Our imaginary novice handler, Babs, was originally motivated to participate in the sport for the external reward of money. But as she was inducted into the practice of agility, her reasons for participating evolved. We can see in her changed outlook a desire to excel in the very particular way that the sport or game of agility demands, by seeking the internal rewards (or goods) of the practice.

What Is a Practice?

The agility handler and her dog do not participate in the sport of agility in isolation from other practitioners. If the novice handler

Five. The Internal Goods of Agility

aspires to improve, she will come to understand that this activity is embedded in a richer context. First, there is the history of agility that is marked by changes and improvements in the sport over time.[2] Second, agility is situated in a social and cultural setting where sport protocol and standards of excellence operate. Third, agility is structured by organizations like A.K.C. and A.S.C.A. These institutions largely administer the competitive aspects of the sport by setting the rules for competitions at sanctioned trials. Finally, within the activity of agility there are esteemed practitioners who train, teach, compete, and judge. These individuals sometimes act as ambassadors of the sport by virtue of accumulating a great deal of expertise over a long period of time: advising, evaluating and, possibly, mentoring those who have less experience. These four features of agility are characteristic of what MacIntyre (1984, 187–88) calls a "practice."

It is only by participating in the practice of agility, i.e., from the inside, that we acquire the relevant experience to identify and to describe the internal goods of the sport. Because standards of excellence are built into the activity of agility itself, practitioners who learn the sport will pursue the activity in conformance to these standards. In particular, acquiring expertise in agility starts with being humble about what we do not know yet. Our own efforts to excel must be subject to review by those practitioners who have more expertise in the sport. For example, MacIntyre (1984, 190) remarks, "If, on starting to play baseball, I do not accept that others know better than I when to throw a fast ball and when not, I will never learn to appreciate good pitching let alone to pitch." It might turn out to be controversial who, in fact, has the relevant expertise in agility. There may be disagreement about this especially as the sport evolves and changes. But one main feature of a practice, per se, is that standards of excellence are not decided by individual practitioners alone, since the authority of these standards is located in the history, social context, and protocol of the practice. In other words, if I run an agility course with my dog, Maggie, and allow her to launch herself off the top of the A-frame, then we do not conform to standards of excellence of the sport no matter what I say about my own performance. Likewise, the dancing camel does not decide herself whether or not she is an excellent dancer. She must subject her dancing to review

Canine Agility and the Meaning of Excellence

by knowledgeable critics who understand what it means to correctly perform a pirouette, for example. Lobel's fable is incomplete about who the critic is and whether or not this critic has the relevant expertise to pass judgment.

When we undertake an activity like agility, we defer to the rules and protocols of the sport that are guided by its history and culture. These rules may indeed come under review over time. But at any given moment there exist standards of excellence to which practitioners conform. Who guides the novice agility practitioner? Those who have the most relevant experience and who are ideally situated to act as *paragons* of the sport. These practitioners will be the best judges of what counts as achieving the internal rewards of agility. Paragons or exemplars are ideally positioned to guide the apprentice. But how does this guidance happen? Here is one illustrative example from my own history of competitive trialing with Maggie.

At a certain point in our competitive struggles the excitement of running courses interfered with our modest ambitions. I was suddenly faced with an over-aroused dog who could not imagine hitting the bottom of the A-frame, stopping on the pause table for five seconds, or holding her start line until I released her. Let's be clear. I created these problems because I did not know enough at the time to predict the consequences. My only excuse is that Maggie is my first agility dog and my first Aussie. I had no idea what I was doing despite the gentle suggestions made by others who watched her performance deteriorate over time. During this period I believed that our problems would never be solved since no matter what I did in practice at home, training there did not transfer to the competitive setting. So I watched other handlers especially closely when they had similar performance challenges. At one point I *believed* that because some people spoke loudly and threateningly to their dogs at the bottom of the contacts—"You stay!!!"—that this is how I should handle Maggie. No. I'm sure I made her fragile grasp of these situations even worse by yelling. But it wasn't until I watched one particular handler and her young dog train the contacts all weekend long, maybe 10 runs altogether, that I saw what I wanted to do with Maggie. This person is not a well-known trainer, nor does she have a reputation for winning classes. But she knew what her particular dog needed: quiet training moments that could be practiced in the ring at a trial and only lasting 45–60 seconds. Over and over again. "This is a happy handler and a happy dog," I thought. And she is creating understanding and trust with her dog right before my eyes. So when MacIntyre suggests that "some [in the practice] are best able to judge and to innovate because they best understand the highest standards so far achieved," this is the kind of example he might have been thinking about. As a novice in agility I have to be prepared to watch, listen, evaluate, and revise my views about who are paragons of excellence in the sport and why. These are not necessarily the handlers who run the most dogs or the winningest dogs. The best practitioners of the sport are not those who speak loudly and threateningly to their dogs to demand compliance. When I reflect about who I would like to emulate in the sport, I watch to see what human and dog teams are happy at the end of the run, no matter what happened out there. I listen for the tone of the handler's voice, inviting her dog to the weaves or tunnels. And I notice when things go wrong. What does the handler do or say to her dog? How does the dog look? Worried? Low to the ground? Moving away from the handler to the exit gate? To me these are signs that a handler is failing to facilitate what I believe are the necessary relational values that characterize excellence in agility.

The Relational Values of Agility

MacIntyre would say that pursuing the internal goods of *any practice* are ultimately made possible by the virtues, such as justice, courage, and honesty. But this level of description is not particularly useful for those of us who practice the sport of agility (although they are good traits of character to cultivate). The virtues that make possible the realization of the internal goods of agility cannot be only human virtues, as I argued in Chapter Three. What is unique about agility that sets it apart from most other practices is that it is a cooperative activity between humans and dogs, so the goods internal to agility are, in part, relational. Think about the ideal bond between any handler and her agility dog. How do we mark this special kind of relationship? I propose that we identify the following values: *mutual*

Canine Agility and the Meaning of Excellence

respect between handler and dog, mutual trust between handler and dog, and mutual communication between handler and dog. Realizing these values defines the relationship between agility handlers and their dogs in the pursuit of the internal rewards of the sport. One way of thinking about this is to say that excellence is an evaluative concept, an ethical concept.

Ethical excellence does not merely *describe* a relationship between a handler and her dog. Rather it is a recommendation about the good. In other words, these relational values of respect, trust, and communication *ought* to be realized in order for excellence to be achieved. Think of it this way. In order to be a good person, we might say that one ought to be honest. Similarly, in order to achieve excellence in agility, one ought to realize a certain kind of relationship with one's dog characterized by mutual respect, mutual trust, and mutual communication. What we aim to capture by a display of excellence in this sense is a certain human-canine relationship that is shared across all those practitioners of agility who are motivated to achieve the internal goods of the practice. As MacIntyre (1984, 193) says, "a practice is never just a set of technical skills ... even when the exercise of those skills may be valued or enjoyed for their own sake." So when respect, trust, and communication are demonstrated by an agility team in this special kind of partnership, then the kind of excellence on display is not merely an exhibition of skill or exceptional performance, although that may be present as well. Rather, it is an ethical performance.

The most convincing validation for the ethical concept of excellence comes from practitioners themselves. If we want to know why we should endorse such an idea, just talk to those who train, compete, and practice agility. Ordinary practitioners of the sport are amazingly eloquent about what they believe is the heart and soul of our sport, and that is the complex training and working relationships that we have with our dogs. This suggests that I am indeed on the right track. But ultimately the ethical concept of excellence gets its justification by imagining what would be left of the sport if we subtracted respect, trust, and communication with our dogs.

To understand this kind of justification, recall what we have said about Babs, our imaginary novice handler and her novice dog.

Five. The Internal Goods of Agility

Initially we lured Babs into the activity of agility by giving her money for running courses competently and, perhaps, cleanly with few or no faults. This was agility done for reasons that are external to the activity. She desired the money and participated in the sport in order to get it. This kind of motivational state does not necessarily encourage or honor any kind of mutual respect or mutual trust with her dog. Babs may believe that the surest way to get paid for her participation in the sport is to use negative reinforcement when handling her dog and punitive measures in training and in competition. And if we are honest, that might actually work for her to become moderately competent and to gain the external rewards she seeks. In fact, if one is motivated solely by external reasons for undertaking an activity like agility, even cheating will be a possible means to acquiring the reward. But I suspect that most agility practitioners will abhor this description about how to introduce new handlers to our sport. That is because most of us share a commitment to excelling in agility in a way that privileges the exquisite partnership we have with our dogs. In fact, if this piece of it were not realized, the sport itself would be unrecognizable. In other words, what characterizes the very nature of the activity are not the external rewards of the sport (recognition, money, status, prestige) but the internal rewards. Those internal rewards do not reduce to technical skills or exceptional performance, even tiny, beautiful moments of brilliance. What is excellent are those relational *values* that exist between a handler and her teammate: mutual respect, mutual trust, and mutual communication. When these values are realized, exceptional performance may also be on display, or not.

Who Displays Excellence?

We've said that most agility enthusiasts are amateur hobbyists. What this means is that the amateur is engaged in what we have called serious leisure. For us agility is a labor of love. But the core concept of excellence applies both to elite performers as well as to novice practitioners of agility. In this sense it is a univocal concept. But I am not saying that everyone who undertakes the sport of

A.K.C. judge Diane Fyfe cheers for a competitor at Southern Adirondack Agility Club (SAAC) Trial at High Goal Farm, August 2023 (photograph by David K. Cerilli).

Five. The Internal Goods of Agility

agility is excellent. This is much too liberal (and implausible). Those who display excellence satisfy the core concept of excellence. This includes practicing or competing in the sport of agility (as opposed to watching) and following the rules of the sport. Further, both elite performers and the amateur hobbyist desire to improve and to acquire expertise and knowledge about the sport we have chosen, not for the occasional "ice-cream pleasures" that it provides, but because we are striving for excellence. The striving is the laborious part of what we do, no matter how unexceptional the outcome. Moreover, agility is a practice, a cooperative activity between humans and dogs. Therefore, aspiring to excellence in agility means more than merely trying to improve according to one's own estimation. Apprentices as well as paragons of the sport seek to realize the internal goods of agility. These goods are modeled by the best practitioners in the sport who exemplify exceptional physical handling skills, imaginative course strategies, working together as a human and dog team, and cultivating mental alertness while in motion on an agility course. Excellence is possible only if these relational values are realized: respect between handler and dog, trust between handler and dog, and communication between handler and dog.

First let me start by identifying some cases that are not displays of excellence and why. Recall that Maggie and I struggled to realize qualifying runs in the U.K.I. online trials (Chapter Two). At that time I temporarily forgot what was best for my dog. Instead I practiced repeatedly to run a trial course until Maggie just stopped working altogether. In hindsight I see that forgetting Maggie's needs and wants is a failure of respect for her. She wants to please me, and she has to be able to trust that I will ask her to do only what makes her healthy and happy.

Recall our story about Rob and Dusty, "the world's least likely agility dog" (Chapter One). There is more than one theme throughout this memoir, of course. But the main storyline captures the idea that Rob is striving for a particular outcome, the external rewards of competitive agility that take the forms of ribbons, titles and championships. Along the way he revels in his status among the club members when Dusty performs well. And when he and Dusty have imperfect runs, he is mortified and distraught. This is an agility

Canine Agility and the Meaning of Excellence

handler who displays what it means to single-mindedly pursue the external rewards of the sport at the expense of the internal goods of agility. What is largely missing from this story is the context: what it is like to try to improve, not merely as measured by a competitive outcome, but also what it is like to communicate in training what is expected of Dusty, and what it is like to try to become a better handler.

Remember my interview with Sue Hall in Chapter One? Sue is reluctant to characterize her practices with Esther as excellent. But I disagree. One example she described as "close to being excellent" is when Esther is "with her," jumping everything, coming to the inside or backside of a jump when cued and, most important, when Esther does not spin before a jump. Sue contextualizes this performance by saying that this may not be perfection, but it is a problem to be solved, a training puzzle about handling and what her dog needs, for example, in order to go straight to the jump from a distance out of a tunnel without spinning. So when they both get this communication right, maybe they are having "an excellent day."

> But who would say I was excellent? Robin [the instructor] could say I was having an excellent day. Maybe if I started doing perfect runs with her. Not even perfect. There's no such thing as perfect. But if I was just hitting and she didn't spin. If I could get her not to spin, I would think I was doing an excellent job with her. But then, we've done it for so long. Can I change that? But I'm not going to quit because she hasn't learned not to spin. Because I probably created it and she has fun with it.

What is remarkable about Sue's explanation is her reticence to call the performance of a practice run excellent. Rather, she focuses on the training challenge or the puzzle created to try to communicate with her dog about a bit of behavior that happens in one or two moments in a longer sequence of jumps. If Sue can figure this out, there will be understanding and communication between her and Esther that is worth celebrating.

In Sue Pietricola's interview (Chapter Two), the idea about excellence is articulated in this way:

> Well, this is my whole thing about excellence, okay? Excellence is a made-up thing that we have in our heads, and we all have some sort of

Five. The Internal Goods of Agility

little image of what we think that looks like. But for every dog and every human being and every dog–human being combo on the planet, excellence looks like something different. So if I see a person who's new to agility and they go out there and they accomplish something new and they have that "I did it" look on their face, and it was a stretch for them, to me, that's excellence.

The example that Sue offers is about a novice dog and handler team:

> I don't know a lot about [X's] students, but I went to one of her workshops. And maybe she [the handler] wouldn't think of herself as being super novice. I mean, maybe she's intermediate. Those labels are not great, but a lot of times this handler doesn't get where she needs to be or put forth her best effort. And her dog is distracted enough doing its own thing. But she had this moment where the dog was connected to her. She sent it through the tunnel. She got to where she needed to be. Ideally, you want to exit on the side of the serpentine that you're going to be going to next. And it was fluid and she got herself there, and it was like this four-jump sequence. But you could just see her saying, "Yes!" It might have been the only really successful thing she did that wet day, but it was beautiful.

With this example Sue is reminding us about how essential connection and communication must be between handler and dog to achieve excellence, even if this is only a moment in a longer sequence of jumps or over many, many attempts to master just one kind of skill.

And finally I want to profile a different story told to me in an interview with Jodi Pangman about trust as an example of excellence (Chapter Four).

> Well, [excellence] for me, I guess, would be with my Toy Fox, who's very noise-sensitive and would often in training just freeze, just stop and freeze. Something startled her, something scared her. But she would just freeze and nothing I did could get her to move. She didn't trust me. She was just frozen. But finally, I guess it was the first time that she trusted me enough to overcome that, she just moved out of that frozen position. I was so proud of her. That was excellence for her. Not so much on my part, but I was proud that she finally trusted me. I'm her soft place to land because that's what I've been doing for the last couple of years,

trying to make her realize "I got you. I got your back. Nothing bad is going to happen out there." Then when it finally happened in training I knew eventually it would happen in a trial.

Jodi's example illustrates what I have tried to articulate throughout this chapter: excellence in agility is far more complicated, and interesting, than mere performance. The ordinary practitioners of the sport who I have interviewed have no hesitation clearly articulating that what is at the center of excellence is this exceptional relationship between a handler and her dog as teammates. We can capture this main idea by saying that excellence is an ethical concept identified by the relational values of respect, trust, and communication.

Do Agility Institutions Corrupt?

What could it possibly mean to say that agility institutions *corrupt* the practice of agility? If organizations like A.K.C. sponsor the practice and activity of competitive agility, then these institutions are positioned to distribute external rewards in the form of titles and championships. Typically there is no money involved, but there is surely status and esteem transferred to those who accumulate accolades sanctioned by agility institutions. MacIntyre says that external goods are "always some individual's property or possession." These goods are "objects of competition" in which some people win and some people lose.

The presence of external rewards in the sport of organized competitive agility is not problematic per se. It is that these kinds of goods may distract from or possibly replace altogether the *internal* rewards of the sport (MacIntyre 1984, 194). To understand this cautionary remark, think about how even local agility competitions are sanctioned by national or international organizations. The local clubs that sponsor these events must be affiliated with a particular institution (A.K.C., C.P.E., and A.S.C.A.) in order to ensure that qualifying runs, ribbons, titles, and championship points are "legally" earned by handlers and their dogs. The worry is not that the internal politics of agility organizations apply unfair or inconsistent standards of excellence. Rather, it is that "the ideals and the creativity

Five. The Internal Goods of Agility

of the practice are always vulnerable to the acquisitiveness [and competitiveness] of the institution" (MacIntyre 1984, 194). The practical consequence of this institutional influence is that even novice practitioners of the sport are steeped in a culture where institution-specific external rewards prevail: pursuing the qualifying run or "Q," chasing the double Q, earning a title, or earning a championship ribbon. I know something about this because I am equally influenced by this culture. No matter what a person says when she comes out of the ring, "I'm just training," "I'm working the contacts," "I'm practicing the [start line, teeter, backside cues]," these remarks are typically just a temporary pause before competing in earnest again to chase whatever points or titles or championships are within reach.

For many competitive agility practitioners of our sport there is nothing amiss in this description. But think more carefully about what we may have given up if the pursuit of external rewards is single-minded and all-consuming. The internal values and goods that characterize "the gentle pursuit of a modest competence" include a passion for getting it right. But remember that for the amateur the desire to improve is relative to each handler and dog team. In other words, those of us who are smitten with the desire to excel in agility may be aiming for improvement but not necessarily perfection. This is because most of us are not elite athletes with high performance dogs! For example, Maggie and I can improve a start line stay, practice difficult weave pole entries, and backside sends, etc., with various degrees of success, but never qualify in the class that we are running. In other words, the qualifying run is not sensitive to and does not reflect these incremental moments of improvement or progress that characterize the amateur agility practitioner's relationship to the sport. Perhaps this gradual refining of skills is marked by a comment like "Well, we did that right, at least." But the small successes are typically overshadowed by the fact that the run did not qualify. For example, when someone asks me how we did at a trial I might point to these small improvements. But perhaps I will add, "I just made a few handling errors that prevented us from qualifying in that run." As if qualifying is the *real* measure of success at the trial. In most stories that we tell about our practice of agility, external rewards like Qs, titles, points, and championships prevail,

Canine Agility and the Meaning of Excellence

sometimes at the expense of honoring the way in which we are "uplifted and brightened" by the activity itself and the relationship of trust, respect, and communication that we have with our willing and hardworking teammates.

Pay attention instead to the momentary gems that we can easily overlook. A young dog sends to a tunnel, understanding the verbal command. A shy dog masters the teeter, trusting his handler in an unfamiliar ring. An over-aroused dog sticks the A-frame contact or a start line, respecting and communicating her understanding of the many moments spent proofing this position. An experienced dog sends out 20 feet to do the weave poles, thereby communicating her drive and enthusiasm. These are not merely technical skills. They are the products of training, time, attention, and mutual understanding communicated between handler and dog. Typically these moments have been preceded by failures and frustrations in trying to improve. Sometimes the difficulty is insurmountable and our goals must be revised. Other times it is persistence, patience, and heart that continues to bring us back to the agility field. But I may be easily distracted from all of this complexity, history, and experience that has fashioned my own particular participation in the sport of agility. This may happen if I focus instead on what most people take to be an essential measure of success and excellence" earning a qualifying run, a ribbon, or a placing at a national event. Recall that Jodi and Ann (Chapter Four) encourage a different way of thinking about competitive performance, especially for novice handlers and their novice dogs. They call it a "personal Q" when the team successfully negotiates part of a course that is challenging.

If I am careful and attentive to the task, the story that I prefer to tell about my passion for the sport is longer and more complicated. It includes many years of training my dog and thinking about how best to go on successfully and happily. There are frustrations and failures we overcame. There are minor but joyous moments of communication and understanding between us. And all of these experiences are relative to my own particular resources, capabilities, and level of interest. This more complex story captures how meaningful the sport is to me, how much I care about improving, and how these aspirations drive and organize events in my life. Being mindful of these contextual details also functions to resist the potentially corruptive influence of agility institutions that shape our participation in the sport by reference to a particular concept of excellence. Because now we can see how inadequate it is to measure the ethical value of excellence in agility by using external rewards alone. Whether or not we qualify in a competitive run or whether or not we display moments of "awe" is secondary to the specific relational goods that bind us intimately with our dogs.

Introducing Diane Fyfe

Diane Fyfe is an A.K.C. agility judge. I caught up with her at the very end of a judging assignment for a three-day agility trial at High Goal Farm. I asked about her experiences in the ring, competing with her own dogs.

The dog I have now that I compete with is a Golden Retriever that I bred. We do obedience and agility. He's four years old and he is in the Excellent division of agility and in the Utility level of obedience. I bred him down from his grandmother and a dog from Vancouver. Anyway, he comes from a lot of working lines. Unfortunately, though, I'm judging so much and judging and teaching and traveling so much lately that I haven't trialed a lot with him. But the good news is he's such a good dog that whenever I do decide to bring him to a trial, he usually qualifies or places. I want to be fair to him, and that's all part of the sport. Unfortunately, because of my choice to be traveling and judging a lot, he's not with me often. It's taking more time for me to accomplish certain competitive goals that other people would accomplish more quickly because they're with their dogs.

What does excellence in agility look like from the judge's point of view?

Well, first of all, in addition to what I just said (being a good teammate and having a good relationship), I think that your ability to recover, not only physically but also mentally, from a mistake that you created in the ring. Handler error happens probably 90 percent of the time. Again, it has to do with trust and honesty. Did I trust my dog? Did I not trust my dog? Did I make too quick of a decision in handling a certain sequence? You have to be honest with yourself.

A.K.C. judge Diane Fyfe is hard at work in the ring, judging a three-day trial for Southern Adirondack Agility Club at High Goal Farm, August 2023 (photograph by David K. Cerilli).

Five. The Internal Goods of Agility

In order to be successful you have to recover from that mistake and move on. This is in the same class, same course. Recover and move on. It has a lot to do with forgiveness.

There was a good example of this at the trial I just judged. Yesterday, a gentleman was having trouble with a blue tunnel, which from the inside looks darker to the dog compared to a lighter acceptable color in A.K.C., like yellow. The dog refused the tunnel pretty much all day yesterday. You have to check the equipment and make sure there's nothing in there. Maybe a dog did urinate or do something in there in the tunnel to turn the next dog off, but nothing was in the tunnel. Today the club decided to change the tunnels to yellow. We couldn't change them in the middle of the day yesterday because it wouldn't be fair to the other competitors. So we changed it today, and, sure enough, the dog went in the tunnel. But here's what happened. The handler at this point is worried. I call this a delayed response. You're worried about the tunnel now no matter what color it is. Yesterday you had trouble. You're thinking you might have trouble today. The dog went in the tunnel pretty quickly, and it was hard for the handler to get over the fact because he was worried about the tunnel. Just in that split second he created a mistake after the tunnel.

He did exactly what I would praise. He forgave his dog for making the next mistake because it was his fault. It was his fault because he was so focused on that tunnel. He was not focused on the next obstacle. He forgave his dog, praised the dog, and just quit. Right there. I don't recommend that you quit because you have to be able to move on and praise the dog and be successful instead of creating a total letdown. Think about all those emotions happening within 60 seconds. Maybe you made a mistake, but you recovered, you got over it, and the rest of the course was successful, perfect. I mean, you executed everything the way you wanted to, so you actually recovered from a mistake that you made. The excellent part of it is the recovery part.

So, in other words, a team can display excellence but fail to earn a qualifying run?

Yes. The other thing I think is that people need to ask themselves how much passion do they have for this? If you really want

Canine Agility and the Meaning of Excellence

to be excellent you have to have a passion for what you are doing. Otherwise, are you going to put 100 percent effort into that thing? Because you're not going to make a lot of money doing this. You're not going to make any money, as a matter of fact. You're going to spend a lot of money. So what are you there for? Are you there for the recognition? If so, that is not the right motivational state to have in the pursuit of excellence.

A good example of this is people who go out and buy a dog that does not fit them. You get a dog because it's the breed that's winning or it's the line of dog that's winning. So you go out and you get this dog just solely for that reason. Or you create a breed. You create a mixture of dogs because you want to win a certain class or you want to win this or that. To me, that's not excellence. You are creating something so you can win and be recognized. But when a competitor is not successful or "recognized" there is a lot of frustration. I see that in the ring as a judge. People start out with this really awesome dog. They go through half the course and it's just beautiful. And then toward the end, something happens that's considered a failure on a course. You see the whole demeanor of that person just dive because they're not being successful. And they don't recover from it at all. Not even when they put the leash on the dog and leave the ring. They just don't recover at all from that. Yeah. It's embarrassing. It's extremely frustrating. They carry it with them outside of the ring in their demeanor and attitude, facial expression and everything.

Do you think that the culture of A.K.C. competition encourages a misguided emphasis on qualifying points, titles, and championships?

I wouldn't say that. I would say that the A.K.C. is a business. It's a well-known dog registry that's grown with the demand of their customers, and their customers love dog sports. And so it's the A.K.C.'s job as a business to organize the rules and regulations, and on top of their list is safety. There are safety rules, all kinds of rules and regulations. But the individual is the one who's responsible for their own behavior. So if you decide that you are going to compete in this venue of A.K.C. Dog Agility, then you need to follow the rules and recognize the fact that in order to have a good time and to be successful, you not only have to follow their rules but also do it with a good

Five. The Internal Goods of Agility

spirit and a level of kindness. You're the one that chose to play in that venue.

I don't see anything that the A.K.C. is doing that encourages the wrong attitude. Now, if you want to talk about something other than dog agility, any sport that you can think of creates the same thing that dog agility is creating. It is that spirit of competition. And some people don't know how to handle that spirit of competition with a level of relaxation and spiritual mindfulness that needs to be there in order to be successful. We decide to get just as antsy, uptight, and worked up as our dog, and some of us don't know how to go into the ring relaxed. That includes being physically relaxed. And you can look at some of these people that go into the ring, they do not look relaxed, including myself at times. But when you do watch yourself, you see some of this stuff too. We're all human. But at least we can recognize what we each need to do in order to work for excellence.

Summary

We began this chapter with a question about standards of excellence. What are these? Where do they come from? And who gets to decide what is excellent in agility? When the dancing camel is criticized for her ballet performance it is tempting to believe that the camel does not display excellence. But who is the critic and what are the credentials of this heckler in the audience? We cannot be sure from the short fable itself. But what we can be sure about is that what counts as excellence in dance as well as in agility depends not on individual preference but on the larger historical, social, cultural, and institutional context in which the activity is situated. Following MacIntyre (1984), we called this a *practice*. Standards of excellence emerge from those who exemplify the internal goods of a practice. So in agility these exemplars might be trainers, coaches, judges, or competitors. Their degree of expertise qualifies them to be "paragons" of the sport, those who are trustworthy, proficient, and have a practical understanding of the internal rewards of agility. The main idea that emerges from understanding agility as a practice is that excellence is an ethical concept. Excellence does not reduce to technical skill, nor

Canine Agility and the Meaning of Excellence

can it be completely explained by exceptional performance. If excellence were only interpreted in this way, then it would be possible to define the activity of agility by reference to the external rewards of the practice (status, money, or prestige). Instead what defines the internal goods of agility is the relationship between handler and dog. Excellence in agility just is the realization of those relational values between handlers and their canine teammates: mutual respect, mutual trust, and mutual communication. Diane Fyfe emphasizes this ethical concept of excellence when she says,

> The biggest part of the sport, in my opinion, is that you're honest with yourself and you're honest with your teammate, and you are fair to each other. That honesty builds trust, and that fairness builds trust, and that would all include keeping both of you in physically good shape and mentally and spiritually in good shape. I think it's very important that you look at what's necessary if you're going to be competitive, especially with another species as a teammate. You have to understand one another pretty well, which means that you have to learn how to communicate with one another and trust one another. The only way you're going to do that is if you spend a lot of time together.

There is still a cautionary reminder in the pursuit of excellence, and that is the organizational culture of competitive trialing. The ethos of competition has the potential to distract from what counts as excellence in agility. This may happen if a competitor exclusively and single-mindedly pursues the external rewards of the sport by investing time and attention into accumulating titles, points, championship ribbons, acclaim and recognition. Diane Fyfe reminds us that it is not agility organizations, per se, that potentially corrupt. Rather, it is the responsibility of competitors themselves to exchange "recognition" for trust, forgiveness, honesty, communication, and spiritual mindfulness in the pursuit of excellence.

Six

Training Excellence

Trainers like to say that you haven't any idea what it is to love a dog until you've trained one (Hearne 1986, 93).

This chapter is about training excellence but it is not a set of instructions about how to make your dog excellent by training. Rather, I want to know how training shapes and contributes to the meaning of excellence in agility. I have already said that ethical excellence is the relationship between handler and dog when it is characterized by respect, trust, and communication. For example, consider these comments by Diane Fyfe, the A.K.C. agility judge I interviewed in Chapter Five. She directs us to look at what comes before the agility run, the training and practice.

> There are a lot of variables to [excellence in the ring]. I would consider myself extremely successful if I'm bringing out a young dog and there's something on the course that I haven't practiced yet with this young dog. So I honestly say, "I haven't done this with my dog. Not sure if we can do this." We go into that sequence and it doesn't work out for my dog and for us as a team. I forgive myself, forgive the team, and we move on to the rest of the course and we complete it successfully because we have practiced and trained and we're honest with ourselves and confident with the rest of the course. To me, that's more successful than actually getting a Q. I also think that a lot of times we aren't honest with ourselves about whether or not we have been training hard enough, if we have been conditioning hard enough, if we warmed up before our run, if we made the connection with our dog before the run, or if we allowed ourselves to get distracted with something else that's surrounding us. There's so many variables that make you successful as you go in the ring. And so some of those things come naturally because you've practiced

them. You go in the ring and everything's old hat. Yeah, we've done all of these sequences before. I have a lot of confidence in my dog and I've warmed up. There's a lot of things to look at to make it excellent.

Sue Hall reminds us that even a moment of excellence in agility has wide scope because it includes what came before in a complex training relationship.

> Of course, [this one handler] is, like, heads above everybody else. When I watch her run her dogs, I think, "Wow, why can't we do that?" But then I understand how it fits into her life and how constant her attention is to training and running those dogs ... the handling skill. The handling skill. The way she and her dogs have a verbal connection. Our dogs have never been that well trained. So this [learning how to do agility] has been, like, eye-opening. Yeah, it is just a marvel. It's the control that they have over their dogs. Or the dog's willingness to be part of it.... But I don't always know what I'm training. What's the dog thinking about to create that behavior?

In order to appreciate how training contributes to the ethical sense of excellence there is a view that we must consider first. Some people might say that dogs have excellence inherently, not because humans have created this quality by training but just because dogs are thinking beings who have their own interests, preferences, and desires. We can imagine this possibility by reading Dion Henderson's children's novel *Algonquin: The Story of a Great Dog* (1953).

A Great Dog

Algonquin is an exquisitely talented Pointer, a birddog who is chosen from a litter of puppies by the narrator as a young boy. He remembers his first glimpse of this puppy, standing by himself and separate from his seven yelping, ear-flapping, roly-poly siblings.

> He was white in the body—not a dark hair, all white to the ears—and his head was solid liver. The head was what you noticed, from the time he was born. You felt somehow, long before you could really tell, that there would be clean, harsh, predatory lines about it. It reminded you a little of a baby eagle, but different—or a young king, but different—of many

Six. Training Excellence

things, but always different, different. Maybe it was his eyes, a little cloudy and undecided, as though he did not know whether he would love greatly or hate bitterly [Henderson 1953, 21–22].

What makes Algonquin a great birddog? Readers understand that Algonquin's excellence is something that the dog has from the very start. Whatever makes him great was there at the beginning, and it blossoms into exceptional talent in the field.

> The birds were where Algonquin was unmatched. He spoke to them in the immortal and universal language that all men and all dogs understand, and the galleries would hush to hear the rolling periods of his classic declamation. When you saw him swinging wide, burning whitely across the bird fields with that blazing speed, to come down on a full wild covey in a locked and statuesque point that skidded him ten yards, pinwheeling across the stubble on braced legs, lofty as a king acknowledging the presence of other royalty, you knew that you had seen what painters see in their hearts but seldom put on canvas [Henderson 1953, 163–64].

Birddogs run hard and fast through rough terrain. Their pads become like leather, the nails wear short, brambles cut the underside of the dog, grasses and weeds wear the hair on the dog's muzzle and tail from brushing through the cover. Is this drive something you can train a dog to do?

> It is a hard life, and it is not mastered by qualities you teach to any dog. He has it bred into him for thousands of years by elimination and for several hundred additionally on purpose, and either it comes down to him strongly enough so nothing stops him or it does not; and there's no use trying to teach him any more than there is trying to make him forget if you do not want him to have it [Henderson 1953, 177].

The story of Algonquin is a good place to start an inquiry about how training shapes excellence because if "there's no use trying to teach him," then it would seem that the trainer plays only a small role in the development of excellence in a dog. I have this on good authority. When Maggie was rehabilitating her tendon injury, I tried to introduce my husband's English Setter to agility. Lukas and I started doing some foundation work indoors and gradually moved outside as the weather got better. Lukas had moments of brilliance. Once he realized that he could chase the flirt pole *after* he jumped a short sequence or ran through a tunnel, he was fast, fast, fast. This seemed so promising, until he spotted a turkey in the woods near the agility ring, or until he froze to point a songbird sitting on the fence, or until a butterfly flitted above his head. Then he was lost to me. No toy or tasty treat would lure him back to agility focus. So I understand what Henderson means when he says about a birddog that "there's no use trying to teach him any more than there is trying to make him forget if you do not want him to have it."

Training Capability

However, consider a competing historical and philosophical view about excellence, one that points in another direction. Aristotle's view about the good life for humans is that excellence or human

Robin Magee's dog, Sequence, is fast through a tunnel. PEN NY-ASCA Trial, Horseheads, New York, September 2023 (photograph by Benjamin Griffith).

Six. Training Excellence

flourishing does not develop naturally. It must be cultivated by habituation and the practice of moral and intellectual virtue over a lifetime. Moreover, excellence for a human being is specific to the function of humans. We must know what capabilities distinguish humans from other animals in order to know what excellence is like for humans as opposed to other living things such as dogs, horses, or plants. Yet in a provocative passage Aristotle says, "Similarly the virtue of a horse makes the horse good and good at running and at carrying its rider and at awaiting the enemy" (Aristotle, *NE* 1106a10–2). This passage is puzzling since here Aristotle does indeed attribute virtue to a horse, but elsewhere he unequivocally states that only humans have the kind of rationality to acquire virtue in the genuine and proper sense.[1] This leads some scholars of Aristotle to say that nonhuman animals do have a kind of virtue (or excellence) that does not depend on having practical rationality or deliberation. What kind of virtue does a horse or dog have?

Schollmeier (1992, 42) argues that some nonhuman animals have "hybrid virtue." This kind of virtue is one that results from the trainer's ability to develop good habits in the animal in order to improve its function and capability. This idea is consistent with what Xenophon says in his writings on equitation. In his treatise *The Art of Horsemanship*, Xenophon writes that the principles of horsemanship are designed to develop and to improve the horse's ability to stop and start all of a sudden (*EQ.* 7.18), to run up and down hills and to leap banks and ditches (*EQ.* 8.1). About the need for training collection in the horse, Xenophon says,

> It is necessary to collect a horse in the turns because it is neither easy nor safe for it to make short turns at full speed, especially if the ground is hard or slippery. When he collects it, the rider must with the bit allow the horse to lean as little as possible, and he must lean as little as possible himself. If not, he must surely know that trivial things will be sufficient to cause both himself and the horse to fall flat [*EQ.* 6.14–15].

Naturally, we want to extend this idea about excellence beyond equine virtue to canine virtue or excellence. If so, we should ask what functions and capabilities of the dog the trainer is interested in improving.

Canine Agility and the Meaning of Excellence

One possible answer to this question is articulated by Vicki Hearne (1994) who argues that the training of animals produces "animal happiness." When Hearne is asked what companion "animal happiness" might be, she replies that a dog and handler discover happiness together in the labor of training. On many accounts of training the assumption is that the dog must submit to the trainer and be compliant with commands or orders. But Hearne articulates that it is through training that dogs may claim rights against humans to demand respect, attention, and response (Hearne 1994, 53). Training a dog is "yearning for excellence" where the talent of the dog is brought to fruition by this relational work. And just as Xenophon articulates that the horse can more exquisitely realize its capability through training, Hearne suggests that animals have the capacity to lead more than merely pleasurable lives. They are capable of leading lives that allow for "satisfactions that come from work in the full sense" (Hearne 1994, 204).

> This happiness, like the artist's, must come from something within the animal, something trainers call talent, and so cannot be imposed on the animal, but at the same time it does not arise in a vacuum....

These remarks allude to the central role that training plays in producing excellence in agility. Since we have now identified ethical excellence as respect, trust, and communication, it is time to clarify how agility training may contribute to acquiring these three kinds of relational goods between handlers and their dogs.

Respect

What does respect look like between a trainer and a dog? In order to emphasize the reciprocal relationship of respect we need to say something more about the dog's mind. Haraway (2003) characterizes training as training *with* dogs, a mutual relationship that involves a cooperative process of education. To watch an agility team at work is not to observe an exercise in compliance but a display of communication between two beings with agency. Agility practitioners and trainers understand that building mutual respect means

Six. Training Excellence

that the lines of communication are open: from handler to dog, and from dog to handler. It is possible for each member of the team to make a mistake. And with this possibility it must be acknowledged that animals (and humans) have a point of view and are capable of learning their respective responsibilities. So mutual respect between handler and dog means "paying attention to and responding to each other" (Lund 2014, 108).

Let me offer an example about how mutual respect may fragment. Maggie is fast on the course and I am relatively slow. This means that I am often not where I need to be in order to tell her what obstacle is next. For other handlers this might only result in a run that is less than neat and tidy. For me this failure to handle efficiently and clearly aggravates my dog. Maggie does not politely manage these ambiguities in a run; she is over-aroused and frustrated by starting and stopping, by late cues, or by getting in her way as she is jumping. This typically means she will jump up and grab my arm with her teeth, producing bruises and sometimes bloody tooth punctures. How are we to understand this kind of failure of cooperation? I have had many training puzzles with my dog over the years, but this is by far the hardest challenge for both of us. The temptation is to scold her on course. Maybe. She does have to understand that biting me is not okay. But this does not get to the root of the problem and it does not credit her with understanding. It is because she wants so badly to do this work that she displays frustration when she is temporarily thwarted. It's as if she is telling me, "Do your part, please! Tell me where to go sooner and more clearly. I just want to run fast and jump." If this is the right reading it says much about her beliefs, her desires and her agency. She is not a robot that operates mechanically by commands I give her. She is an emotional rocket off the start line with a clear idea about what we are doing in the ring and how the run should go. The solution to this problem is a work in progress. The way I see it, we must each become responsible for doing our designated jobs. I must get better at handling; she must become more tolerant of my mistakes. Working her more at a distance is the best training strategy for now. This way I can stay away from her teeth.

If we read the philosophical literature about respect and non-human animals, the training relationship between handler and dog looks very different. In a classic and much discussed book about animal rights, Tom Regan (1983, 243) argues that some nonhuman animals deserve respect because they are "subjects-of-a-life." To be a subject-of-a-life means that an individual animal has beliefs, desires, perception, memory, and a sense of the future. Moreover, that individual animal has an emotional life that includes pains and pleasures, an interest in his or her welfare, and a kind of agency by which the animal may initiate action to pursue his or her interests or goals. If a particular animal does have the capacity to display most or all of these characteristics, then that animal has "inherent value." And if an animal has inherent value then it deserves to be treated with respect. In fact, the animal has a *right* to respectful treatment. This bit of reasoning marks the philosophical origins of the animal rights movement.

I think it is not exaggerating to say that there have been volumes written about the plausibility of Regan's argument and the moral implications of our standard practices involving animals.[2] For example, some domains of concern inspired by Regan's work include whether or not we should use animals in scientific experimentation, whether or not we should eat animals for food, whether or not keeping animals in zoos is morally permissible, and whether or not pet-keeping is morally defensible. In turn, a wide variety of criticisms target Regan's argument. These typically cluster around the crucial but vague concept of inherent value, unclarity about which animals do or do not qualify as subjects-of-a-life, and what counts as the right to respectful treatment. Since we are discussing respect, in particular, what does respectful treatment entail in Regan's view? As Henry (2013, 100) describes it, Regan's argument about animal rights entails that the animal's inherent value "must never be compromised for some other goal we might set for ourselves, no matter how worthy." So, for example, if a particular person has a passion for agility, the training and practice that goes into pursuing this sport may well violate the animal's autonomy and agency. After all, the dog has not chosen this activity and may well want to do other things like chase squirrels or Frisbees.

This is not the place for a philosophical discussion of the animal rights literature. However, we should note how radically the

Six. Training Excellence

philosophical analysis of respect for nonhuman animals pulls apart from the animal trainer's understanding of what respect means. Hearne (1994, 35) describes training a dog as moving to the point at which the dog is a full partner or friend. But the dog and the person must "earn the right to friendship." Having rights against one another is an altogether different relationship, one that is predicated on mutual respect. Consider the example of Kathy Kaegel and her support dog, Remington.

> Kathy Kaegel has no arms or legs. Her dog therefore has an extra-tough task opening doors for her, and an extra degree of responsibility, since she cannot correct or control Remington.... So it may look on the face of it as though Remington is a slave—some have said that all dogs are slaves. But you get a different picture watching Kathy Kaegel brush her dog every day, not merely patiently but with pleasure, with a brush held in her teeth.
>
> Watching dogs like Arrow and Remington, and thinking about the mutual autonomy and mutual dependence that is the miracle of our friendship with dogs, I have this advice for anyone who wants a dog. Before you get the dog, find a good trainer. One who gives the feeling that he or she knows what it is for a dog to be reliable enough to cooperate with someone who has no arms and no legs, and one who also knows what it might be to honor and motivate so reliable a companion by brushing her with a brush held between the teeth [Hearne 1994, 35].

Trust

There are two main characters in the movie *Rescued by Ruby* (Shea 2022). Daniel O'Neil is a state trooper who has struggled to join the state police K-9 search and rescue team. He has failed to qualify many times for one reason or another, and he is facing his last opportunity to be admitted. Ruby is a Border Collie that has been sent out for adoption seven times and has been returned to the shelter each time. The families claim they cannot control her or train her. She barks wildly, tears up pillows, and digs holes in the garden. When we meet her at the start of the movie she has exhausted her welcome at the shelter. So when Daniel learns there is not enough

Canine Agility and the Meaning of Excellence

money available to buy a trained German Shepherd for search and rescue work, he ventures to adopt Ruby and train her to the task. Initially this does not look promising. Since Daniel and Ruby are not admitted to the training class, they must work on their own to prepare for the six-week test. The most inspiring parts of this story center on trust and the violation of trust, or betrayal, between Daniel and Ruby. This emerges from their training relationship: what Daniel has taught Ruby, what Ruby has learned, and how their partnership is defined by cooperation and understanding.

When Daniel and Ruby take the search and rescue test to qualify for the K-9 team, Ruby is tasked with finding three objects in 30 minutes: a cell phone, a firearm, and human remains. She finds the first two in record time, and then they move inside the building to search for human remains. We watch tensely as Ruby searches the hallways, offices, and stairways. Finally, she comes to Daniel and sits directly in front of him. "What's she telling you?" asks the commander. "No remains here," answers Daniel. The commanding officer of the team asks Daniel if he is sure. If there is one mistake they will not pass. "If she says it's not here, it's not here," replies Daniel. In that moment Daniel displays his trust in his dog: what she knows and her sense of responsibility for the job she has been trained to do. This is not blind trust. It is shaped by the partnership they have forged together as a team in training. So there is judgment here as well. Daniel knows his dog. He judges her to be honest and thorough in the search. Ruby makes a judgment too. She tells Daniel unequivocally that the object cannot be found.

In her philosophical discussion of trust, Annette Baier (1995, 151) wonders how we develop the skill to make judgments about whom to trust. Sometimes trust in people is based on a snap judgment as when we ask a stranger at an airport to watch our bags. Maybe we base this judgment on a combination of eye contact, clothing, or tone of voice of the stranger. But other judgments about trust are actually well informed. This trusted person may be a friend, an ally, or a colleague that has demonstrated concern for our welfare on other occasions. Baier acknowledges that we even trust animals by putting ourselves in their power but she does not elaborate about when this kind of trust is warranted. There is always the possibility

Six. Training Excellence

for trust to be misplaced, between people and between trainer and dog. This is so because mutual trust requires cooperation. Usually cooperation between people may be realized through speech that reveals complex intentions, beliefs, and feelings. But when cooperation and trust is achieved between trainer and dog, there must be something beyond speech that signals that each is trustworthy. Consider this scenario about the betrayal of trust.

When Ruby and Daniel are called to search for a missing person, presumed dead, the K-9 team gets their first chance to display their skills. Ruby is sent to search. She actively ranges through the house and eventually barks to indicate a "find" outside on a slightly raised wooden deck. Daniel and the other officers scan underneath and find nothing. "You have to make the call officially, Daniel." Daniel checks again, looks at Ruby and pauses for another moment. He is clearly frustrated and surprised. Finally, he says, "No body." Viewers do not understand yet that Daniel's judgment is actually a failure to judge correctly or a betrayal of trust. But what else can he do? He believes that his honest, reliable dog has made a mistake. But he blames himself as well. It's as if his self-confidence is so eroded that he can't imagine that his dog has fulfilled her responsibility. The most devastating outcome, he believes, is that Ruby will clearly not be on the K-9 search and rescue team and neither will Daniel. His disappointment transfers to Ruby. "Go on," he says to her as she presses her nose against his hand.

Why is this a betrayal of trust? We find out later in the film that a body was found buried in three inches of concrete under the deck. The commander is in awe that Ruby could have scented this body at all. He says to Daniel, "You made the wrong call. You should have trusted your canine." The film engages in what may be a fanciful depiction of the cost of the betrayal of trust. Ruby disappears, and Daniel searches in vain to find her in a storm. Perhaps this did not actually happen in the true events that inspired the film. I'm not sure. But the storyline certainly profiles how judgment about when and whom to trust occasionally fails. Moreover, when we experience a betrayal of trust, there are unexpected emotional consequences.

Trust is not always good and right. It is not a virtue to trust per se. This is so because when we do trust some other person, animal, or institution, we make ourselves vulnerable to risk. This becomes especially problematic when there is inequality of power. It is the trainer's responsibility to take care of the dog she trains. But remember that we humans get to say when and what our dogs will eat, how they will exercise and for how long, and what games or sports we will play with our dogs. This means it is possible to make incorrect decisions about what is in the best interest of our dogs. In other words, by virtue of this inequality there exists the potential for harm.

> By cooperative trusting behavior the truster renounces some of her own small power to control matters, and as long as the more powerful trusted one wants what the truster wants, this voluntary renunciation of control will advance the truster's goals, will get her where she wants to be, and will often help her to increase her own strength and ability. When matters work out well, her voluntary giving up of power will be an investment whose returns will be an ultimate increase for her. But if things go badly, she will be harmed, not helped, by her trusting. Risk is of the very essence of trust [Baier 1995, 196].

When dogs trust us they put their welfare in our hands to make discretionary judgments about how to preserve their physical safety and emotional health. It is not always obvious how best to honor this trust. For example, when I entered Maggie in the U.K.I. online trials, my zeal for posting a perfect qualifying run blinded me to Maggie's welfare. She did not want to run the same sequence over and over again. She voted with her paws, refusing to jump an obstacle that was right on her path, sniffing the ground instead. Baier (1995, 138) remarks, "To trust is to let another think about and take action to protect and advance something the truster cares about, to let the trusted *care for* what one cares about." So there are good grounds for feeling dismay about my online trialing because I did not in that moment protect Maggie's welfare and her happy, enthusiastic participation in the sport of agility. In any case, I learned my lesson.

But some agility handlers do demonstrate that they have earned their dog's trust to keep them safe. Jodi Pangman (Chapter Five) described a moment of excellence that involved trust when her Toy Fox would freeze during a practice run or during at a competitive trial. When she finally overcame this moment, Jodi remarks, "I was

Six. Training Excellence

proud that she finally trusted me. I'm her soft place to land because that's what I've been doing for the last couple of years, trying to make her realize, 'I got you. I got your back. Nothing bad is going to happen out there.'"

Mutual trust between a trainer and her dog is mysterious. It cannot be articulated by merely saying, "I put my trust in you." This suggests that we should look beyond verbal language to identify *gestures* of trust. These inter-species cooperative practices might be displayed by bodily motions and facial expression: the resigned shoulder shrug, bowing of the head, encouraging smiles, raised eyebrows, or direct eye contact or avoidance of eye contact (Baier 1995, 176). Baier identifies these "natural rituals" as those that are recognized between parents and infants, but they are also more conventional, like the handshake. As Baier puts it, "The handshake, that sacred sealer of deals, is a nice example of a gesture that combines trust and caution" (197). As a greeting the handshake implies "equality, reciprocity, and goodwill." But what could possibly stand in for the handshake in training a dog? What natural or primitive gestures can be shared across species that represents mutual trust, equality, and cooperative activity?

Communication

When Salty, a one-year-old Pointer, comes to Vicki Hearne for training, she has exhausted her owners. Her instinctive dedication to finding and pointing birds at this stage of her life just means "going hard and tirelessly." Her owners merely fuss as she knocks over furniture, eats off the kitchen table, or jumps through windows in pursuit of meadowlarks. Hearne takes her time with Salty. At first it is just the command "Sit." As Hearne describes, "Salty, sit!" is not yet language. Salty obeys Hearne, but Hearne doesn't obey Salty.

> One day, though, and quite soon, I am wandering around the house and Salty gets my attention by sitting spontaneously in just the unmistakably symmetrical, clean-edged way of formal work. If I'm on the ball, if I respect her personhood at this point, I'll respond. Her sitting may have a number of meanings. "Please stop daydreaming and feed me!"... [I]f I

Canine Agility and the Meaning of Excellence

respond, the flow of intention is now two-way, and the meaning of "Sit" has changed yet again. This time it is Salty who has enlarged the context, the arena of its use, by means of what we might as well go ahead and call the trope of projection. Salty and I are, for the moment at least, obedient to each other and to language [Hearne 1986, 56].

According to Hearne, training provides a vocabulary that allows trainer and dog to communicate. Training develops ennoblement, character, and a sense of responsibility and honesty in both dog and handler. The word "responsible" is often the most appropriate word to use to make sense of the animal who is trained. This is the word that "makes sense of the situation."

> The better trained a dog is—which is to say, the greater his "vocabulary"—the more mutual trust there is, the more dog and human can rely on each other to behave responsibly.... A good police dog has not only a large vocabulary but also extraordinary social skills. He understands many forms of human culture and has his being within them. He can be taken to the scene of a liquor-store robbery and asked to search, with the handler trusting that he won't molest the customers or other police officers or the clerk behind the counter. He knows what belongs and what doesn't, sharing our community and our xenophobia as well. He can take down a criminal who is attacking his handler on Monday and on Tuesday play with the patients at the children's hospital [Hearne 1986, 21–22].

What does training do for the dog and the trainer? It makes the relationship "coherent" in that both learn to speak the same language. Mastery of novice obedience commands means that we have formed a *society* (Hearne 1986, 67). And what does incoherence in training look like in our society? It means that a dog like Maggie can't understand what is meant in a new situation or in a new context. She might believe that a send to the backside of the tunnel means jumping on or over the top of the tunnel because my shoulders and feet are pointing that way. In fact, she did do this when my cue was incorrect. It's as if she was saying, "Well, we have never jumped *over* the tunnel before but maybe this is what she wants today." She is trying so hard to comply, but it just doesn't add up because I haven't been clear or consistent about what I want. When

Six. Training Excellence

we do communicate and there is an established vocabulary with my dog we are transformed. There are little glimmers of understanding between us when we run fast and clean; these are like sparkling gems. I can conjure up cases when I have said "out" in time for Maggie to know to jump out away from me. Or when I say "tunnel" two or three jumps away from the entrance and she drives ahead with confidence and enthusiasm. I have in mind a magical, very long off-leash recall when Maggie runs back to me as fast as she can, ears pressed flat against her head and her mouth open, tongue hanging out, for the sheer joy of it.

And what is the contrasting conception of training? Some might think that it is force, coercion, brutalizing, or even just discouraging the dog or the horse to perform the desired behaviors. I guess there is always the possibility of bad training and bad trainers who rely on techniques that flatten or dampen the soul of the animal. But if you do coerce your dog, then you will never achieve with them what is done at the highest levels of training. You end up with something dull and lifeless. When Hearne (1986, 163) characterizes understanding between trainer and horse, for example, she means that there is a "single supple relation" in the high-level dressage horse or the Grand-Prix jumper. A better description of this relation is "artistry" where the movements of the horse are "fluid," "expressive," and "brilliant" (Hearne, 1986, 160–61).

What does artistry look like between an agility dog and a handler who have developed a "single, supple relation"? Is it like when I say "close" to bring Maggie to the off-side of the tunnel, and she reads my word and my body to perform this new task? What a burst of love and delight I have for her in that moment. Does she feel it too? When she exits the tunnel, she barks and growls and jumps wildly. And then I find the ruff on her neck and bury my hands in there, shaking her head back and forth gently. "What a good, smart dog you are," I say as she growls back at me. She's excited and ready for more. More of what? Does she want to just go off and run through more tunnels on her own? Maybe at the beginning of our agility education, yes. But now she wants to do this with me: tugging on a toy, running fast, jumping, and most of all just interacting with me, stringing together short moments of communication, and celebrating these.

Canine Agility and the Meaning of Excellence

Introducing Robin Magee

I'm sitting with Robin Magee at Aussie Acres Agility where Robin lives, trains her own dogs, and teaches all kinds of students and their aspiring agility partners.

Introduce yourself and your family of dogs.

I live in West Chazy, New York. And I own Aussie Acres Agility. I train, teach, compete with three Australian Shepherds right now. In the past I've had seven Aussies, a Papillion, Collies and a Sheltie. That goes way back but you can't talk about the dogs today unless you talk about the dogs yesterday, right? Because one builds on the other. The one you have today is preparing you for the one you have tomorrow. I have Synchrony, who is seven and a half years old. And he is a lot of dog. He's been my most vocal dog, and when I got him, he was my fastest and most pushy. But he loves training and working in agility. It's his passion which is really fun because my dogs before him were

Robin Magee and Solar display opposite motion handling. Syracuse Obedience Training Club (SOTC) A.K.C. Trial, Syracuse, New York, February 2023 (The Spotted Tongue Photography).

Six. Training Excellence

slower, steadier, but consistent. And then Solar will be six in January. I got him after I lost one of my Aussies at the age of seven. So Solar came after him. And he's my first tailed Aussie which I love. The tail is more than steering. It definitely shows a lot of emotion. And then Sequence, who is now 20 months. Already Sequence is probably the most experienced in understanding this sport because he's gotten all of the benefits of what I have learned and taught my other dogs through their lifetimes, and he's gotten that in 20 months. We do still have a long way to go. He loves agility in a different way than Sync. If he knows we're going to play something and I have his ball, he's like "Just tell me where to go." He's like a herding dog looking at the sheep. "Tell me what to do. I'm on it." That's his look. Solar's more easy-going. He's not super-fast but he's honest. You have to be pretty clear with Solar because he's a thinker. And Sequence wants to be right.

How did you start doing agility?

So when I got my first Aussie, Sidney, I wanted my dog not to be just a good pet, but I wanted him to have skills and good training. I did a little bit of obedience with both the Collie and the Aussie. And then there was a group that was meeting in a horse barn. My dog knew nothing about agility. And we just stood in line and waited for our turn. And then we asked our dogs to do it, and they did it. No training, no nothing.

I think I liked doing the sport with my dog. It was a different challenge than obedience because the dog was being physically challenged and not just mentally challenged. They have to jump, and they have to do that in association with the handler. This is the funniest thing. I'm standing in line with my Aussie at that first agility class, and other people asked, "How long have you been doing this?" And I said, "Well, this is our first day." And my dog was doing everything I asked him to do. He was really biddable. "Okay, you asked me to do this, so I'll do it."

As a trainer and as a competitor, what does mutual respect look like between a handler and her dog?

I think the respect comes out of trust because it's no different than in human relationships. If you do this for me, and I trust that you'll do this for me, and there's some type of reward in it, then it helps build the relationship. So it's almost like respect and trust are so intermingled that it's hard to separate them, right? I mean, you bring that puppy home and into your house, and you're training with this puppy, whether you're going to do obedience or agility or just have a family pet, that process begins immediately and you're starting to build trust. So if they pee in the house, you don't want to break down your trust by spanking your puppy. You want to make sure you take them out and reward them for peeing outside, and then they'll be more apt to do that again. So you're building trust as you go along. And I would say respect comes out of trust. Respect the other because you believe that they're going to be honest with you. I can trust that if I ask my dog to do something, they will trust that I will give them the right feedback. And then they have respect for me and I have respect for them. That helps the relationship grow and grow. So it's like making a cake. You have to put in certain ingredients to have the end result. I think what's great about dogs is that we've always said that they have never-ending love for us. Even if someone is bad to them, they will still love that person. They're very trusting of us that we have their best interest in mind, even if some people actually don't. That is amazing because if another person didn't treat you well, you would walk the other way. Dogs don't tend to do that.

But I think when you're training and you're teaching something new to your dog, you have to understand what your dog is understanding. You have to have a good eye for this in order to reward the dog in the right way and at the right time. You can't get mad at them because they don't understand. I think respect grows out of that. The trainer has to understand that dogs are not humans; they think differently and they understand differently. In fact, every dog understands things differently. I see that every day when I teach. I always ask, "How do I communicate with this particular dog?" That's respect on [the trainer's] part, right? So you're being respectful by saying they're different than me. They understand differently than me. I have to figure out how to communicate what I want so that they will learn.

Six. Training Excellence

So what does successful communication look like between a handler and her agility dog?

You have to create a way of communicating with your dog in order that he can trust that what you're saying is really what you want. I've had students who get frustrated: "Well, I showed up for my dog. My dog didn't show up for me." But wait a minute. Sometimes people feel that the dog and the handler have to give exactly the same amount in agility. And a student will become frustrated if it feels a little bit like she's giving all of herself and maybe the dog is not giving all of herself. But I don't think it's always 50–50. I think that when dogs are in the training process you have to give more. It's not always a 50–50 relationship. Sometimes I think the dogs are giving more than the handlers, and sometimes the handlers are giving more than the dogs. If I'm teaching something, it's not 50–50. I'm taking 75 percent of it, and they're doing 25 percent. And then there are times like at the last trial when Sync was on fire. He was doing his 75 percent of the activity, and I'm just trying to catch up. So I think you have to understand that the relationship scale goes back and forth. But when your dog doesn't understand and is not feeling that trust, then you have to be the one to give more because the dog's not able to.

Because dogs don't speak, and the way they communicate is different than ours, I think it's on the handler to be aware of how dogs understand and how they communicate. When a dog's wagging his tail because you're saying "good boy," they understand that. That's one way of communicating. But I guess I often think of communication and agility as being able to give all the right feedback to them so that they are able to negotiate the course effectively the way you want. If you have a really good run where you felt like you couldn't have done anything differently, and everything was just the way it should have been, then I think your communication at that point was spot on because your motion was appropriate, your position was appropriate. All of your input was communicated exactly. So the dog says, "Got it. Got it. Got it. I know exactly what you're saying." That's what I am striving for.

Miscommunication is when the dog's taking the wrong side of the jump, or we're just not getting it and they end up dropping the bar because I'm not showing the right information. And then you take that step back and you say, "Okay, I should do this instead." You have to take a step back and say, "What does my dog really need?" And then you add that information. "Wow. Now I've just communicated."

I just tell Sync, especially, "If you would give me a lead out, I could have told you where we were going. We weren't going there. But you didn't give me the chance because you were just a rocket man." Oh, my God, he's funny.

What does mutual trust look like between a handler and her agility dog?

For example, Solar loves his ball. If I pick up his ball, he will trust that I will throw it to him. If he takes some obstacle, he knows he'll get rewarded by me throwing the ball. I feel like his independent obstacle performance is great because he trusts that when he goes out to the weave poles, I'm going to give him a reward for it.

I think that that's what I try to encourage with my students because my dog will always go out and do something I ask because he trusts that I am going to reward him for it. Most handlers don't trust their dogs to be independent because they feel like they have to be a part of it. There's a two-way street, mutual trust. I trust my dog will go do that tunnel, and my dog trusts that I will give him a reward for doing that tunnel. That's how we play and train. It's a way of living.... These dogs are not just agility dogs. They live in my house. They sleep on my bed. They sit with me on the couch. We go running together. We spend a lot of time outside together and doing things together. They follow me around the house like I'm the leader of the parade. When they are puppies that relationship is built up over time. It's like this is a pyramid, right? You have that foundation in the way we live together, and then you can put on another layer, maybe a little bit of training, and then you can put another layer on, and another layer over that. You keep adding the layers until you have a complete 20-obstacle course because you have built that relationship all the way up.

It sounds like what you are saying is that a good trainer has to understand the dog's point of view. So you have to know a lot. You have to

Six. Training Excellence

imagine things from the dog's point of view in order to know how to train. Does that seem right to you?

You have to spend time watching them and listening to them and understanding them because they are not human. Some people believe and act as though dogs have human traits and personalities. They may have some, but they're dog traits and personalities. When people say, "Oh, my dog is punishing me." Well, maybe not. But when handlers get in the situation where they might think more about the Q and showing off for their friends or getting titles, they forget that this is still a dog and they don't care. They're not human. You can't say, "I need you to follow the numbers, and I need you to do a back side on number three, and I need you to stick your two on two off, and I need you to do all this." He's a dog. That doesn't mean anything to him. People who have only been doing agility for four or five years may not really see that training and understanding, building communication and a trust relation grows over time. It's not something

Robin Magee's dog, Synchrony, is airborne over this jump. Syracuse Obedience Training Club (SOTC) A.K.C. Trial, Syracuse, New York, February 2023 (The Spotted Tongue Photography).

that you're going to have when you first start. But that's why you have to be patient.

Summary

We started this chapter about training excellence with the story of a great dog named Algonquin. This birddog is seemingly excellent from the very beginning of his life. As some might say, he is naturally great. Perhaps. But there is another historically credible point of view about how excellence emerges in humans and animals with the assistance of teachers and trainers. Aristotle argues for such a view in order to explain how human flourishing depends on developing those capabilities specific to human beings. And Xenophon profiles examples about horsemanship where horses and their human handlers can develop exquisite skills in partnership with a trainer. Hearne argues that animal happiness involves just this kind of potentiality. Training a dog or a horse attests to "the capacity for satisfaction that comes from striving, from work, from fulfillment of possibility." To be more specific, excellence in agility is made possible by training in order to realize the ethical values of the sport: mutual respect between handler and dog, mutual trust between handler and dog, and mutual communication between handler and dog.

In the next chapter I ask a practical question. What kinds of stories should we each tell about our respective practice of agility in order to magnify and to celebrate the ethical concept of excellence? The stories we tell each other about who is excellent, and why, have the potential to shape the very nature of the sport.

SEVEN

How to Tell a Story About Excellence

In what does the unity of an individual life consist?
The answer is that its unity is the unity of a narrative
embodied in a single life (MacIntyre 1984, 218).

It is time to review the concept of ethical excellence that has emerged from previous chapters. Agility practitioners who display excellence are amateur hobbyists who engage in serious leisure, a labor of love that is driven by the desire to improve and to acquire expertise and knowledge about the sport we have chosen. Further, these individuals practice or compete in the sport of agility (as opposed to watching) and follow the rules of the sport. The core concept of excellence is univocal since it applies both to elite performers as well as to novice practitioners of agility. This is because both elite performers and amateur hobbyists strive for ethical excellence, a value that is characterized by respect between handler and dog, trust between handler and dog, and communication between handler and dog. In other words, ethical excellence is not the same as, and is not reducible to, exceptional performance. Since agility is a practice—a cooperative and social activity between humans and dogs—aspiring to excellence in agility means more than merely trying to improve according to one's own estimation. The internal goods of agility are modeled by the best practitioners in the sport who exemplify exceptional physical handling skills, imaginative course strategies, working together as a human and dog team, and cultivating mental alertness while in motion on an agility course. Moreover, if we seek validation for this particular conception of excellence, we need only talk with agility practitioners themselves. They will eloquently explain that what is distinctive and worth celebrating about agility is the unique relationship that we each have with our dogs who are our partners and teammates in the sport.

Throughout this inquiry I have used stories and anecdotes to explore what it means to realize excellence in agility. Now it is time to focus the lens on the stories themselves. What explanatory value do stories have in general? And why tell stories about agility in particular? The answer to the more general question is that the stories we tell about our own lives provide a connecting unity. MacIntyre (1984, 205) claims that a *self* is "the unity of a narrative which links birth to life to death as narrative beginning to middle to end." Telling the story of my own life allows me to identify who I am by the characters that I play in these stories, and the stories that we tell ourselves and those we tell to others reveals what matters most to each of us. By means of narrative we describe our passions and our aspirations for the future. I argue in this final chapter that the kinds of stories that we *should* tell about excellence in agility have the potential to shape the very nature of the sport. I leave the reader with five practical recommendations about how to tell a story about excellence in agility. Story-telling should include (1) the context and primary intentions of the handler; (2) an answer to the identity question "Who am I?"; (3) an explanation about how the story resists false and misleading conceptions of excellence; (4) *authentic* descriptions of the inner life of your dog; and (5) how a narrative quest for excellence shapes what is good for the sport of agility. But first consider a short hypothetical vignette about a handler and her dog.

Intelligible Behavior

Suppose our imaginary handler Babs sends her dog over a jump, through a tunnel, and then through six weave poles. This activity looks pretty familiar to most of us and we would probably say that we understand what Babs is doing. But consider some possibilities that are consistent with this bit of behavior. Babs is getting exercise. Babs is trying to get ready for a competition. Babs is practicing a certain kind of handling turn. Babs is restoring confidence to her dog. Babs is trying to spend less time alone by participating in a social activity. Babs is trying to socialize her dog by bringing her to agility class. Of course, she could be doing some combination of these; they are not all mutually exclusive. But what this imaginative exercise suggests is that Babs' behavior is not explicable without knowing more about her intentions. We want to hear how she herself answers the question "What am I doing and why?" If we find out that Babs wants to make friends by going to agility class, then her behavior is explained by this intention. It makes her behavior intelligible. But there is more to be said. To correctly characterize her behavior in the agility ring we also have to situate her action in a setting or a context. Babs will only perform this action of sending her dog through a short sequence of jumps if she also has the belief that the practice of agility is a good activity for making friends. In turn this depends on a history about Babs. Why does she want to make friends? How exactly has this social need manifested? Is she recently a widow? Or, alternatively, does her husband believe that she should get out of the house more? If so, then she is trying to make friends in order to please her husband and so on. It is only when this history and context is specified by a collection of intentions and beliefs that we can accurately characterize what Babs is doing.[1]

The main point is that the intelligibility of Babs' action can be captured only by a certain kind of story, one that MacIntyre (1984, 209) describes as a story that "flows from an agent's intentions, motives, passions, and purposes." Moreover, in order to identify Babs' *primary* intentions we ask whether or not she would continue to run her dog in an agility class if she did not believe that this activity would enlarge her circle of friends. In other words, the primary intentions of any agent are those that capture her essential beliefs about what she is doing and why.

Narrative Arc

Each agility practitioner has a story about what she is doing and why that spans our respective participation in the sport. For many people this history of participation extends over many years and many dogs. For each of us a single moment of agility in that history can be located somewhere on a narrative arc: first dogs, novice handler, experienced handler, old dogs, over-aroused dogs, injury to a dog or the death of a beloved agility partner, injury of a handler or a family crisis, new puppy to train. Consider, for example, how my own beliefs and intentions about what I am doing have shifted over time. Perhaps initially I believed that signing up for an agility class was a way of learning a sport with my new puppy. I also believed that doing agility was a good way to focus her mind and a good way to discharge some of her inexhaustible energy. Later I believed that participating in agility class was a way to be competitive. So my primary intentions were to practice agility in order to compete. This soon gave way to problem-solving. At that moment in my involvement with agility, I wanted to use my agility class to fix problems in the ring in order to have more success in competitive trialing. More recently my participation in the sport is characterized by my desire to bring Maggie back from injury. When I run a short sequence in practice or even when training at a trial, my primary intentions are to sustain her physical health. Now as I write this I am just grateful for her presence with me in the ring. This activity that I have such an unrelenting passion for suddenly seems so delicate; it can unravel in a moment if I look away. Notice that each setting and context shapes and influences my answer to the question "What am I trying to do?" The narrative arc of my story about agility is an individual historical account that includes my beliefs, desires, and intentions to act over time.

> It is because we all live out narratives in our lives and because we understand our own lives in terms of the narratives that we live out that the form of narrative is appropriate for understanding the actions of others. Stories are lived before they are told—except in the case of fiction [MacIntyre 1984, 212].

We can see evidence of the narrative arc of agility in comments by other practitioners as well. Robin Magee (Chapter Six) remarks, "You can't talk about the dogs today unless you talk about the dogs yesterday. Because one builds on the other. The one you have today is preparing you for the one you have tomorrow." Diane Fyfe (Chapter Five) connects what is happening in the ring on a particular run with what came before. "Have you practiced this sequence? Have you trained? Are you warmed up? Do you have a young dog? Are you connected with your dog?" All of these questions help to formulate what a particular handler is trying to do at a particular time. This is the context that makes a moment of agility intelligible. Diane Fyfe says,

> I would consider myself extremely successful if I'm bringing out a young dog in the ring, and there's something on the course that I haven't practiced yet with this young dog. I might say honestly, "I haven't done this with my dog. Not sure if we can do this." We go into that sequence and it doesn't work out for my dog and for us as a team. I forgive myself, forgive the team, and we move on to the rest of the course and we complete it successfully because we have practiced and trained and we're honest with ourselves and confident about the rest of the course.

Making the handler's intentions explicit in a narrative history is central to recommending a certain kind of story about excellence in agility. This is so because ethical excellence in agility is not an accidental feature of the activity. It should be the *primary intention* of practitioners of our sport in such a way that it includes specification of the relational values of the activity and the context in which it is situated. This makes the practice intelligible to those within the practice as well as to those outside of it. It's a way of saying, "This is what matters. Pay attention to this kind of story that profiles the ethical relationship with your dog: respect, trust, and communication."

<u>Recommendation 1.</u> Tell a story about excellence in agility that describes a narrative arc. Include your primary intentions for a particular bit of agility behavior (joining an agility class, running a sequence in practice, training in a public park, or running a course or a sequence at a competitive trial). But also include the context of your behavior that situates what you are doing in a longer history of your life. For example, I am trying to improve Maggie's contact performance at this trial because...

Who Am I?

Remember the story about Rob and Dusty, "the world's least likely agility dog"? The characters and the storyline are iconic. Rob

Canine Agility and the Meaning of Excellence

Robin Magee's dog, Solar, flies over the dog walk. Syracuse Obedience Training Club (SOTC) A.K.C. Trial, Syracuse, New York, February 2023 (The Spotted Tongue Photography).

is engaged in a heroic quest for an agility championship. He is like Don Quixote, the character in Cervantes' (1605) novel who struggles mightily to become a knight and to restore chivalry. Quixote's challenges are imagined, his attempts are misadventures, and his "successes" are fiascos. And so it goes with Rob and Dusty whose exertions are real enough but not sufficiently fruitful to accomplish "glory." But we can see that although the quest is thwarted, what survives these comic and tragic outcomes is Rob's relationship with his dog. The narrative arc veers to one side in order to restore what really matters in this memoir. The point is that stories tell us who we are, what role we play in a setting, and the nature of our relationships with others and with our dogs. MacIntyre (1984, 216) says,

> I can only answer the question "What am I to do?" if I can answer the prior question "Of what story or stories do I find myself a part?" We enter human society, that is, with one or more imputed characters—roles into which we have been drafted—and we have to learn what they

Seven. How to Tell a Story About Excellence

are in order to be able to understand how others respond to us and how our responses to them are apt to be construed.

If you haven't yet read the memoir by Jennifer Finney Boylan (2020) titled *Good Boy: My Life in Seven Dogs*, you really should. Boylan's story tracks her own life through the dogs she has owned. It is not about the unconditional love that dogs have for us but about the love that we have for them "and the way that love helps us understand the people we have been." Boylan begins her story as a young boy with quiet and unexpressed yearnings to be something so very different. She ends her story as a middle-aged woman with a family who weathered this transition with her. So we get to know the emotional highs and lows of the author as she "takes the measure of the people [she] has been" by meeting her dogs. There is a Dalmatian named Playboy that Boylan owned when she was a young boy, an overweight "mournful" Dalmatian named Sausage that Boylan owned as a hippie adolescent, a mutt named Matt with a voracious sex drive, a Lab named Brown obsessed with eating her paws, a wise Gordon Setter named Alex who protected Boylan's children and, later, a Retriever named Lucy who scorned the entire family.

> It was Lucy who was on duty the day I finally came down the stairs in heels. She looked me up and down with exhaustion. *Ugh*, she said. *I wish the Lord would take me now*. Actually, a lot of people reacted like that at first, including many of the men and women I had loved most [Boylan 2020, 4].

If stories tell us who we are, then this poignant memoir is a way of marking who Boylan is from the inside point of view, a series of vibrant snapshots of her life as she transitions through difficult but loving relationships with friends, family, and her dogs. Nonetheless, Boylan continues to be the same person who can tell the story from beginning, to its middle, and to somewhere near the end. The narrative arc marks significant moments in this chronicle of her life.

MacIntyre (1984, 216) asks, "Of what story or stories do I find myself a part?" To answer this question makes all the difference in how we think about excellence in agility. Recall Jodi Pangman's remarks about excellence and the mark she wants to make in the sport (Chapter Four).

Canine Agility and the Meaning of Excellence

I just want to do my own personal best. I set my own personal goals and then I try to accomplish them. My thing has always been doing something with a breed that's not a breed you look at and say, "Oh, they're agility dogs." That's the mark I want to make. I just think it's all about the bond you have with your dog and how close you get to your dog. Every journey and every agility trip you take with a different dog is different, and they all teach you something new.

<u>*Recommendation 2.*</u> Tell a story about excellence in agility that profiles who you are as a trainer or as a competitor and the particular relationship that you have with your dog. How would you describe this relationship? What does the story reveal about your passions and your aspirations? What does it reveal about your dog and his or her participation in the sport of agility? What new insights have you learned with a particular dog, past and present? And what matters most about the activity you have undertaken together?

The Explanatory Value of Stories

Stories about people and what they do can have immense explanatory power. For example, some stories have the potential to educate and to shape the reader's understanding about what matters ethically. The methodology of *narrative ethics* uses stories to reveal what is ethically relevant, to "motivate morally good action," and to "guide morally good action" (Nelson 2001, 36). In my book *Food Justice and Narrative Ethics: Reading Stories for Ethical Awareness and Action* (Dixon 2018), I used stories to profile issues of oppression and inequality that cluster around food: how it is obtained, how it is produced, and how it is eaten. A more accurate description of the topic is *food injustice.* In this book I wrote about how marginalized populations suffer from food insecurity but still endure moral blame for not having enough to eat. I wrote about how our food is grown in the fields where migrant farmworkers suffer oppressive working conditions, low pay, sickness, and personal humiliation while at the same time they are targeted and blamed for their own ill-health and poverty. And I wrote about obesity and the way in which public health policy blames individuals

Seven. How to Tell a Story About Excellence

for making poor food choices, rather than a ubiquitous food system that surrounds the eater with cheap but poor nutritional food choices. In all of these settings the memoirs, documentary movies, and podcasts did most of the explanatory work. What I mean is that stories about individual people have the potential to disclose the background conditions that impede actions and truncate opportunities to live well. And the value of these kinds of stories is that we may focus the "ethical lens more accurately on existing injustice, unfairness, and inequality" (Dixon 2018, 5). In this way we position ourselves to be advocates for change.

So there are two general conditions that a story ought to satisfy in order to have this kind of explanatory value. First, a story should openly reveal a target of resistance. It should have the power to lay bare an explanation of how things are that is unjustified, misrepresentative, or false. And second, the story should profile a competing way of looking at the issue to offer an alternative understanding, one that has a better claim on the truth. The stories I used about food justice satisfied these two conditions. They revealed a common misunderstanding about inequality in the food system; I called this the personal blame narrative. This kind of story attempts to explain why populations are food insecure, why migrant laborers live in poverty, and why there is an obesity epidemic by morally blaming individual people. This is the view that I urged readers to resist. The "counterstory" depicted a different explanation that is closer to the truth.[2] These oppressive conditions are the outcome of an unequal distribution of material resources and opportunities that affect populations disproportionately. This is a systemic explanation that forces the reader to reevaluate the personal blame narrative.[3]

We can appreciate the explanatory value of stories in Vicki Hearne's (1986) discussions about training animals. The critical target of these stories is often a confused idea about what good training is and what it does for the dog. In some cases Hearne argues that the dog may be ruined by cruelty or even excessive kindness. Or sometimes Hearne targets academic theories that denigrate the potential for what she calls the "moral transformation" of dogs and horses through training. The story alternative, or the counterstory, allows the dog to be redeemed by a trainer, one who understands the animal and establishes a working relationship that amounts to "justice" for the dog.

For example, Hearne writes about a "true life" dog story involving Rinnie and his handler, John Judge, both members of the Wichita, Kansas, police department. "Rinnie's nose was foolproof, his heart gallant, brave and dedicated, his mind alert and questioning." Chuck Smith reported to the police that he had been robbed and kidnapped in his own car. Rinnie and Judge were assigned to track down the kidnapper who exited the car. When Rinnie was asked to search, he sniffed the car carefully and then walked around to where Smith (the presumed victim) was standing and bit him in the seat. Of course, his handler was appalled, and Rinnie was disgraced. After an investigation it was decided that Rinnie would have to be suspended from the police force. Hearne (1986, 26) writes,

> It is important to notice that the mistake was conceived of as an extraordinarily clumsy one, unworthy of "the most inexperienced police dog." This matters because it indicates the depth of the loss of faith, the darkness of soul, of the moment when John Judge reprimanded Rinnie. When a police dog bites a victim, the perdition of the handler is absolute. The center does not hold, things fall apart. The dog's potential for virtue, and for lapse, is greater than the policeman's for lapsing from human law.

But as you might guess there is more to this story. Another detective assigned to the case began to investigate Smith's background. He ordered Smith to take a lie-detector test which he failed. It turned out that Smith and an accomplice planned the robbery together. So the dog (and the machine) said he was lying. As Hearne tells this story, "order is restored" because it reaffirms Rinnie's honor and acknowledges the moral significance of his actions.

> The fact that animals are so generous in answering us is what makes it not only okay to train them but a human duty, one way we enact our gratitude to the universe that animals exist. It also makes the telling of animal stories that are the genesis of the courage of the trainer part of our duty... [Hearne 1986, 265].

Recommendation 3. Tell a story about excellence that does some explanatory work. Be specific about those ways of thinking about excellence in agility that are misrepresentative or false. Explain how your story profiles the ethical conception of excellence with an emphasis on the relational values between handler and dog: mutual respect, mutual trust, and mutual communication.

The Role of Fancy

When the "Nature-Faker" controversy captured the attention of the popular press during the early part of the twentieth century it was most obviously a debate about the literal truthfulness of the wild animal story. What emerged from nature writers such as William Long, Ernest Thompson Seton, Charles Roberts, and Jack London

Two Corgis (Thisby, left, and Seamus) owned by Sue Pietricola playing in the snow in a chilly -4 degrees. Grand Isle, Vermont, January 2019 (photograph by S. Pietricola).

during this period was a new literary genre: the "realistic animal story." These stories showcased individual animals as the main characters. They were often written from the animals' point of view and made transparent their mental lives, including how they learned, reasoned, and felt emotionally. Even though these stories were wildly popular, they were not intended to merely entertain readers but also to educate. As Thomas Dunlap (1998, 238) puts it, the realistic animal stories were "presented not as fiction or fable but as the fruits of nature study backed by science." What made these stories especially controversial was their declared truthfulness. Seton (1901, 9) begins his "Notes to the Reader" in *Wild Animals I Have Known* by saying, "These stories are true. Although I have left the strict line of historical truth in many places, the animals in this book were all real characters. They lived the lives I have depicted, and showed the stamp of heroism and personality more strongly by far than it has been in the power of my pen to tell."

John Burroughs (1998, 132) led the attack on Seton and Long when he published "Real and Sham Natural History" in the *Atlantic Monthly* (March 1903). "[I]n Mr. Thompson Seton's *Wild Animals I Have Known*, and in recent work of his awkward imitator, the Rev. William J. Long, I am bound to say that the line between fact and fiction is repeatedly crossed, and that a deliberate attempt is made to induce the reader to cross, too, and to work such a spell upon him that he shall not know that he has crossed and is in the land of make-believe." What kinds of descriptions are best for understanding not only what animals are like but our relations to them? Burroughs (1912, 360) believed that science and poetry should go "hand in hand." They each have a contribution to make to our understanding, but the task of each discipline is distinct.

> Science is impersonal and cold, and is not for the heart but for the head. The heart symbolizes so much for us, it stands for the very color and perfume of life, for the whole world of sentiment and emotion—a world that lies outside the sphere of science.

John Burroughs would have us believe that seeing and understanding what animals are like is distinct from, even an "enemy" of, literature and narrative. But this presupposes that understanding animals

Seven. How to Tell a Story About Excellence

is a narrow kind of investigation, one where we might merely record the number of legs on a beetle or the wingspan of a butterfly.

The contrasting position is William Long's recommendations to the nature student to use her insight, imagination, and human sympathy in order to really *see* animals as "luminous" living things as opposed to "stuffed specimens." Long (1998, 144) distinguishes between science, or what he calls "the world of description," and storytelling about animals characterized as "the world of appreciation." Scientific descriptions of animals classify and catalog these according to general principles. For example, we might classify a mouse as a "long tailed" or a "jumping" variety. But what is left out of such descriptions, Long reminds us, are the individuals. The individual mouse's actions may be interpreted by poets, prophets, and thinkers who will reveal more truth about this particular mouse than science can reveal, "as emotions are more real than facts, and love is more true than economics" (Long 1998, 145).

Long is suggesting here that a more accurate and truthful depiction of animals is captured only by a certain kind of narrative, one that singles out individuals as actors going about their daily lives. Scientific descriptions provide us with accounts that are true of kinds of animals; for example, their eating and hunting habits and whatever behavior is common to all members of a species. But such accounts fail to capture the idiosyncratic truths about individual animals. Imagine if we were to write about a human life by resorting to generalized descriptions that are true of all or most human beings; for example, that human beings walk on two legs, eat meat or vegetables but not stones, and so on. Of course, we would concede that such a description is factual, but additionally we can see how much is left out. What is missing is an account of how it is for an individual person to live a human life that includes *her* experiences, what motivates her, and what fears, loyalties, hopes, and loves figure into the living of her particular life. According to Long, the stories that we tell about individual animals are crucial to the authenticity of the account and crucial to capturing the real qualities of individual animals. Long (1998, 147–48) puts the point eloquently in this way:

Canine Agility and the Meaning of Excellence

There is one other thing that the modern nature-writer has learned, namely, that in this, as in every other field of literature, only a book which has style can live. And style is but the unconscious expression of personality. Not only may the personal element enter into the new nature-books; it must enter there if we are to interpret the facts truthfully. Every animal has an individuality, however small or dim; that is certain.... And the nature-student must seek from his own individuality, which is the only thing that he knows absolutely ... to interpret truthfully and sympathetically the individual before him. For this work he must have not only sight but vision; not simply eyes and ears and a note-book; but insight, imagination, and, above all, an intense human sympathy, by which alone the inner life of an animal becomes luminous, and without which the living creatures are little better than stuffed specimens, and their actions the meaningless dance of shadows across the mouth of Plato's cave.

What is striking about Long's recommendations to the nature student is the demand for narrative style in the articulation of *authentic* descriptions of animals. Because the subject of inquiry is an animal, a living thing, we are in danger of getting it wrong about what animals are like if we do not employ narratives that are infused with imagination and sympathy. How can this be so? In what way do stories and the fancy of our imagination bring us closer to understanding the animal mind? For Long, the role of fancy in narrative is to bring us face to face with the *living* animal. By telling or listening to a story about the life of an animal, we achieve an intimacy of description that is meaningful and truthful and, according to Long, more authentic than other kinds of descriptions that merely "catalog" the behavior of an animal. "The truth is, that he who watches any animal closely enough will see what no naturalist has ever seen. This is the simple secret of the wonderful cat story, or the incredible dog story, to be heard in almost every house. It means that, after you have catalogued dogs perfectly, you still have in every dog a new subject with some new habits. Every boy who keeps a pet has something to tell the best naturalist" (Long 1998, 146).

<u>Recommendation 4.</u> Tell your story about excellence in agility by including *authentic* descriptions of your dog. In other words, allow your narrative to be about the individual animal that you know

so well, and tell this story with sympathy and imagination in such a way that the "inner life of [your dog] becomes luminous."

The Ethical Value of Stories

I have been arguing that the core concept of excellence is an ethical concept, one that includes the relational values of respect, trust, and communication. But what I owe the reader is an explanation about what it means to say that some stories about excellence in agility have ethical value, and why we should choose to profile these kinds of stories especially to those within and outside of the agility community. Let me start with MacIntyre's (1984, 219) remark that "the unity of a human life is the unity of a narrative quest." What MacIntyre means is that the ultimate success or failure in a human life can be understood by the stories we tell about what we are seeking. A "narrative quest" must therefore identify some conception of the good for humans. And this will be true for the practice of agility as well. Rather than solely seek the external rewards of the activity of agility (recognition, status), we ought to seek what is good for the sport of agility. This conception of excellence is tied more intimately to the ethical relationship that handlers have with their dogs. So the narrative quest for agility practitioners is characterized by the stories that we tell about our sport which reveal this ethical core concept.

There are three reasons for telling stories about the quest for ethical excellence. One reason is that the relational values of agility are realized in so many different ways. Recall Sue Pietricola's comment, "But for every dog and every human being and every dog human being combo on the planet, excellence looks like something different." In other words, there is not one way in which a particular handler and dog team displays mutual respect, mutual trust, or mutual communication. In the telling of a story, the context may be different from the one in which I play a role, the history of the relationship depicted in a story may be different from my relationship with my dog, and the primary intentions of the handler articulated as part of the story may be dissimilar from my primary intentions.

Canine Agility and the Meaning of Excellence

In other words, what makes a bit of agility behavior intelligible may vary across handler and dog teams, and even for the same team from one day to the next. So the proliferation of stories allows us to envision the many possible ways in which ethical excellence in agility may be realized and sustained. We need these examples in order to imagine the possibilities about what we are seeking.

The second reason for undertaking a narrative quest is that telling stories among ourselves, and listening to what other practitioners have to say about ethical excellence, has the potential to identify obstacles that interfere with realizing excellence in agility. MacIntyre (1984, 219) says,

> [I]t is clear the medieval conception of a quest is not at all that of a search for something already adequately characterized, as miners search for gold or geologists for oil. It is in the course of the quest and only through encountering and coping with the various particular harms, dangers, temptations and distractions which provide any quest with its episodes and incidents that the goal of the quest is finally to be understood. A quest is always an education both as to the character of that which is sought and in self-knowledge.

What "dangers, temptations, and distractions" interfere with our quest for excellence? There are many. Just from my own experience I include the following physical and mental challenges:

- How do I ensure that I can communicate with an over-aroused dog?
- How do I recover psychologically from competitive failures?
- How do I recover trust with my dog after competitive disappointments?
- How do I continue to participate in the sport when my only dog is injured?
- What is my role in the sport of agility if my competitive aspirations are not primary?

Finally, there is a central reason for profiling stories about ethical excellence in agility; such stories are critical to the essential nature of the sport itself. We have to wonder what agility would look like if the relational values that characterize ethical excellence were

Seven. How to Tell a Story About Excellence

absent altogether. Imagine a practice session or a competitive run with your dog marked by disrespect, for example. The central reason that explains why many of us love this activity is that we participate in a partnership with creatures that are autonomous, capable of having beliefs, desires, anxieties, fears, and a complex agency. The heart and soul of our sport can only be sustained by acknowledging the *value* of this complex relationship that we have with our dogs. This is why I believe that the concept of ethical excellence is foundational to the very nature of the sport itself. This is also why I believe that telling stories about ethical excellence is a responsibility of each practitioner of our sport, irrespective of competitive success or exceptional performance in the ring.

<u>Recommendation 5.</u> Tell a story about excellence in agility that describes what is *good* for the sport. Ideally, this should be done by identifying the challenges that need to be overcome in order to achieve ethical excellence. In this way we are each positioned to better understand the goal of the quest for excellence.

"Muster Dogs"

My last illustrative story is not one about agility. It is a four-part reality show on Netflix titled *Muster Dogs* (Boughen, Browning, and Wallace 2022) about herding dogs in Australia. "Whatever for?" you might ask. One reason for profiling this documentary about training "muster dogs" is that there are few films in the public domain about training animals at all, so we should take this opportunity to do some analysis. And for anyone interested in working dogs it is a delightful series. Second, before I end this analysis about excellence I would like a chance to demonstrate that the ethical concept I have articulated is nimble, with the potential to apply more widely to human and dog relationships beyond the sport of agility.

The first episode of *Muster Dogs* introduces the main characters and the training challenge for the five trainers who participate over 12 months. The main breeder of a litter of Kelpie pups is Joe Spicer. He works with a well-known trainer of herding dogs, Neil McDonald. Mr. McDonald has run a training school for 30 years. Mr. Spicer has

Canine Agility and the Meaning of Excellence

bred two of his best working and award-winning trial dogs. He now has five puppies that he will give to ranchers who already use Kelpies to handle their stock. The challenge is see if each rancher and skilled stock handler can train the puppy successfully to meet four milestones of training in 12 months for the honor of the title "Champion Muster Dog." Joe Spicer has put a lot of thought into how to match up the puppies and the ranchers, trying to ensure that the dog's nature aligns with the trainer's nature and the kind of work that they must do as a team. Training a herding dog usually takes three years, so this is an experiment to see if there is a faster and smarter way to train a muster dog. All the stock handlers involved agree that using dogs to move large herds across vast distances is preferable to using machines to do this kind of work. The dogs do not frighten the stock, for example, and the use of animals is more economical and sustainable. Typically, a good Kelpie herding dog will cost anywhere from $20,000 to $35,000. So the incentive is powerful to demonstrate that a rancher can raise and train this kind of dog to be part of a working team of 10 to 20 other dogs. The evaluators hope that they will gain some insights about how the natural instincts of these well-bred working dogs are affected by environment and the different training systems of each of the five handlers. In other words, what training system provides consistency and reliability?

There is quite a lot to this story but I want to focus my comments on a particular trainer who stands out from the beginning as exceptional. His name is Frank Finger. Frank has been raising cattle in Queensland for 45 years, although he is the first in his family to use dogs. He has eight muster dogs before he receives his new puppy who he names "Annie." Frank has trained many dogs so he knows how important it is to spend time with this new puppy in a social way in order to establish a connection or a bond. You can see evidence of this right away as Frank meets his new puppy in the first episode. As well he tries from the start to train respect for the livestock, not applying too much pressure by working too close. He wants his working dogs to create calmness in the stock and not be disruptive to their management. Typically, Frank will wait for two years before he puts a young dog in the big pasture with a lot of cattle, but this challenge will accelerate the training. What I like about watching Frank and his puppy

Seven. How to Tell a Story About Excellence

is how soft his voice is, even when Annie is on the wrong track. He spends time asking for eye contact with her and is always calm. "If you show respect, you'll get the best out of an animal," he says.

The first challenge is when the puppies are four months old. At this time there are seven milestones expected from trainers and their dogs:

- the team must display a bond or "Bluetooth connection";
- the puppy must drag a three-meter rope (without chewing or playing with it);
- the handler must be able to pick up the puppy and keep him or her calm;
- the puppy must be able to participate in communal feeding with the rest of the working dogs;
- the puppy must be able to walk calmly on a loose lead;
- the puppy must be calm on the chain when in the buggy; and
- the puppy should respond to his or her name and come to the handler.

What the trainers call a "Bluetooth connection" is an abbreviated way of describing the bond that trainers are hoping to cultivate with their young dogs. With no rope or lead this joining is a "wireless" connection. This just means that the puppy acknowledges the trainer and focuses attention on the trainer when asked to respond. Neil McDonald advises one handler who is having some problems building this relationship with his puppy. "Try to build the bond without taking too much control over the dog. Don't try to strip the herding instinct and personality out of the dog." When we watch Frank and Annie, it is clear what this looks like. Frank sits quietly with Annie in his lap. He says her name and she looks intently and adoringly into Frank's face and eyes. When she does so, he rewards her by softly saying, "Lovely dog." This kind of milestone demonstrates that the puppy wants to be in the trainer's company. Once you have that connection, the handler and dog team can do anything. Annie will be expected to help herd thousands of cattle in a 10,000-acre paddock. "We do it slowly here," Frank says.

At the six-month milestone the young dogs are expected to show some good instincts for bringing the livestock to the handler.

Canine Agility and the Meaning of Excellence

They also must be able to walk off lead without running after the stock, be able to jump onto the bike or buggy that is used to move the herd, and to demonstrate some basic herding skills such as holding a small number of stock against a fence in a corner ("corner bubble") or on two sides against a flat fence line ("one half bubble"). Annie is exceptional at this evaluation point as well. The off-lead walking sounds rather straightforward, but for these dogs who want so badly to work the stock, restraining themselves to stay with the handler is hard. In another team we see the pup running uncontrolled after sheep, biting and chasing, and generally creating fear and chaos in the herd. Annie, on the other hand, demonstrates that she can apply just enough pressure on the stock to move them quietly and hold them on the fence. She works closely enough to keep them under control and is brave enough to stand her ground but stays a safe distance out. Frank occasionally tells her, "Annie, over" to remind her to work a bit farther away, but she basically just glides around the small herd with just the right amount of pressure.

At the nine-month assessment, the young dogs are really expected to show their skills with livestock. They should be able to stay connected with the handler even in the face of distractions. When working the stock they should be obedient to the handler's commands to "sit," "stop," or "hold." They should be able to work a slightly larger group of stock from both sides and perform a 50-meter cast around the herd. When Annie displays what she can do at this stage, she is brilliant. Frank trains her early each morning for about 10 minutes, adding five head of cattle to the herd each week so that she gradually gets experience with larger groups. She is a wiry and graceful dog. Frank believes she is easy to train and easy to bond with. She responds to Frank's command to "stop" and "down," giving the stock relief from her pressure, and she can work the herd from side to side to bring them to the handler. The 50-meter cast is supposed to send the dog a long distance around the herd. Here Annie works a bit too closely, failing to kick out wide enough initially. But she still passes the milestones with style. Frank believes that she is almost ready to join the big pack of muster dogs.

The final assessment takes place when the dogs are 12 months of age. The young dogs are expected handle a large herd of cattle

Seven. How to Tell a Story About Excellence

on their own to bring the stock to the handler through a gate. They must demonstrate compliance with a "sit" or "stop" command, come when called, and only work the stock when told to do so. The evaluators hope to see confidence, reliability, and precision in managing the herd and to follow commands on the first call. The dogs must be at the right place at the right time at every moment of the task. When all of the teams meet to perform this last challenge, one participant says that the most rewarding feature of the experiment is to see how the bond between trainers and their pups has developed. And Frank and Annie are recognized for having the strongest bond of all the teams. Annie is a settled dog. She is respectful of the herd but also applies pressure when it is needed. She hangs on Frank's every word as she moves around the mob of cattle, tucking them in a little tighter. She sits, backs off, and sits again when Frank tells her. She is calm, sensible and mature, working both the front and the rear of the herd with little fuss and a lot of style. The evaluators agree that Frank and Annie have achieved this level of skillfulness because they have such a deep bond and Frank has followed the training program closely. Of all the teams, Annie has the best manners and the best connection with Frank as she smoothly circles the herd. Of course, Frank and Annie win the "Muster Dog Challenge."

Surely there is something in this documentary about training dogs that speaks to agility practitioners everywhere. It is on display in the quiet and *respectful* working relationship that Frank has with Annie. It is demonstrated by *trust* and confidence as they manage a job with "little fuss and a lot of style." And it is illustrated by the subtle forms of *communication* between Frank and Annie in the work that they do together. "Lovely dogs. With me."

Summary

We sometimes lose track of what matters in the sport of agility. We aspire to performance outcomes: perfect runs or maybe just perfect moments in the competitive ring or in practice. We aspire to recognition, "brags," or respect from friends, coaches, and the agility community. We covet qualifying runs, titles and championships.

Canine Agility and the Meaning of Excellence

All of this is part of the sport and it is part of being competitive. But if these aspirations are all consuming, then we may simply forget that the unique quality of agility is the exquisite relationship that we have with our dogs. This aspiration is never exhausted, although it may retreat from our first thoughts about what we are doing as we place our dog at the start line and get ready to run. I myself am guilty of this failure; it's so easy to get lost. This is why I urge agility practitioners to tell contextually rich stories about what we do. Tell a story that includes the arduous and complex history of training your dog, trying to get better, and developing your expertise in the sport. Be sure to let the rest of us know what you are trying to do in such a way that you profile the mutual values of respect, trust, and communication with your dog. Include in this story who you are as a trainer and as a competitor and what you have learned doing this activity together with your valued teammate. Use the story to resist a misleading or a false idea about training, competing, and practicing agility. Replace this misrepresentative story with one that demonstrates what is good for the sport and what is closer to the truth. By all means tell a story with narrative style that depicts the inner life of your own dog with imagination and sympathy. And this final recommendation may be the hardest of all. Allow your stories to include the obstacles you have faced in the quest for ethical excellence. Acknowledge your successes, but also your defeats, mistakes, revised goals, and your hopes to do better.

Chapter Notes

Chapter One

1. See, for example, Russell (1999) (2004); Simon (2000).
2. Dixon (November 2020). "Maggie's Online Trials" was first published by *Clean Run—The Magazine for Dog Agility Enthusiasts.*
3. See, for example, Bad Dog Agility Podcast, "Why Agility?"
4. *Ibid.*

Chapter Two

1. See American Kennel Club Mission Statement.
2. See Australian Shepherd Club of America, Agility Program.
3. Philosophy of C.P.E. "For the dog and competitor to have fun while successfully competing for performance titles as a cohesive unit, achieved through positive training and teamwork" (Canine Performance Events).
4. See, for example, online dog training courses, books and DVDS offered by Clean Run Productions, LLC; Bad Dog Agility Academy online training and podcast; and online training courses offered by Fenzi Dog Sports Academy.
5. See Nagel (1979).
6. See Carr (2002).
7. See, for example, Robert Simon (2007).
8. See Aristotle, *Nicomachean Ethics* (1099a33–b6).
9. Of course, the problem of causal determinism does not go away this easily. It might be that the moral character of a person is out of her control as well, determined by events that occurred before she was even born.

Chapter Three

1. Dixon (December 2020). "Life Lessons: Agility is Not Just Something We Do on the Side" was first published by *Clean Run—The Magazine for Dog Agility Enthusiasts.*
2. One of my neighbors who saw Maggie being walked by the thief phoned the police department with this information. Then he proceeded to print *laminated* flyers and posted these on the telephone poles near the house where she had been seen. Five years later this good citizen still walks by our fence to greet Maggie, treating her like the queen of Plattsburgh. He's a hero to our family.

Chapter Four

1. For an extended discussion of this fable, see Dixon, B., and Charles List (2013).
2. Aristotle would say that activities "done for their own sake" are leisure activities that contribute to the

Chapter Notes

development of virtue. For example, Aristotle identifies music as an art that will be educative for acquiring virtue (*Politics*, bk. VII, chap. 5, 1340a6; see List (2013, 28–31). See also Stebbins (1992) for a discussion of "serious leisure."

Chapter Five

1. This example is modeled after one described by MacIntyre (1994, 188). MacIntyre invites us to imagine an intelligent seven-year-old child who is taught to play chess. The child has little desire to learn the game though she does have a desire for candy. If she is offered candy in exchange for learning to play competently (even winning), then she will receive the candy. Consequently, the child is motivated in a particular way to learn to play the game. The candy functions as an "external reward" for learning to play the game of chess, in contrast to what MacIntyre calls the "internal rewards" of chess and relevantly similar activities, namely, "analytical skill, strategic imagination, and competitive intensity."

2. For example, in 2016 the A.K.C. suspended the use of the collapsed tunnel. See Lowrey, S., "The History of Dog Agility: The Evolution of the Fast-Paced AKC Sport."

Chapter Six

1. See Aristotle, *NE* 6.1, 1139a6–11.
2. For a sample of this literature see, for example, Linzey and Clark, eds. (2004); Sunstein and Nussbaum, eds. (2005).

Chapter Seven

1. This example is modeled on one that MacIntyre (1984, 206) describes about gardening.
2. For an explanation of a counterstory, see Nelson (2001, 67); Dixon (2018, 6–11).
3. A fuller explanation of this argument can be found in Dixon (2018).

Bibliography

"Agility Grand Champion—Recognizing a Lifetime of Excellence." 2018. American Kennel Club. Accessed December 7, 2023. https://www.akc.org/expert-advice/news/agility-grand-champion/.

"A.K.C. Mission Statement." n.d. American Kennel Club. Accessed December 8, 2023. https://www.akc.org/about/mission/.

Aristotle. 1985. *Nicomachean Ethics*. Translated by Terence Irwin. Indianapolis: Hackett.

"ASCA Agility." n.d. *ASCA* (blog). Accessed December 8, 2023. https://asca.org/competitive-programs/agility/.

"Aussie Acres Agility." n.d. Facebook. Accessed December 7, 2023. https://www.facebook.com/aussieacresagility/.

Bad Dog Agility. 2018. "Play Before Work." *Bad Dog Agility* (blog). May 29. https://baddogagility.com/play-before-work/.

Bad Dog Agility. n.d. Accessed December 8, 2023. https://baddogagility.com/.

Baier, Annette C. 1995. *Moral Prejudices: Essays on Ethics*. Cambridge: Harvard University Press.

Bierce, Ambrose. n.d. "The Devil's Dictionary, Online & Unabridged." Accessed December 7, 2023. https://thedevilsdictionary.com/.

Booth, Wayne. 1999. *For the Love of It: Amateuring and Its Rivals*. Chicago: University of Chicago Press.

Boughen, Michael, Sally Browning, and Dave Wallace, dirs. 2022. *Muster Dogs*. Four episodes. Netflix.

Boylan, Jennifer Finney. 2020. *Good Boy: My Life in Seven Dogs*. New York: Celadon Books.

Burroughs, John. 1912. "Science and Sentiment." *Independent*, February 15.

———. 1998. "Real and Sham Natural History." In *The Wild Animal Story*, edited by Ralph H. Lutts, 129–43. Philadelphia: Temple University Press.

Campos, Daniel G. 2014. "Skills." In *Bloomsbury Companion to the Philosophy of Sport*, 369–71. Bloomsbury Companion Series. London: Bloomsbury.

Canine Performance Events (CPE). n.d. Accessed December 8, 2023. https://cpe.dog/.

Carr, David. 2002. "Where's the Merit If the Best Man Wins?" In *Philosophy of Sport: Critical Readings, Crucial Issues*, 197–205. Upper Saddle River: Pearson Education.

Cervantes, M. [1605] 2003. *Don Quixote. A New Translation by E. Grossman*. New York: HarperCollins.

Clean Run Productions, LLC. n.d. "Dog Agility Training Products, Dog

Bibliography

Agility Online Training." Accessed December 8, 2023. https://www.cleanrun.com/.

Crank, Jennifer, Sarah Fernandezlopez, and Esteban Fernandezlopez. n.d. "Handler Mental Recovery after Canine Physical Recovery." Bad Dog Agility. https://baddogagility.com/category/podcast/.

———. n.d. "Why Agility?" Bad Dog Agility. https://baddogagility.com/category/podcast/.

Dewey, John. 1934. *Art as Experience*. New York: Berkley Publishing Group.

Dixon, B.A. 2008. *Animals, Emotion, and Morality: Marking the Boundary*. Amherst, NY: Prometheus Books.

Dixon, Beth A. 2018. *Food Justice and Narrative Ethics: Reading Stories about Ethical Awareness and Activism*. London: Bloomsbury Academic.

Dixon, Beth. 2020a. "Maggie's Online Trials." *Clean Run* 26 (11): 28–29.

———. 2020b. "Life Lessons: Agility Is Not Just Something We Do on the Side." *Clean Run* 26 (12): 10–12.

Dixon, Beth A., and Charles J. List. 2013. "Breaking the Rules of Respect." In *Respect: How Do We Get There? A Philosophical Inquiry*, 59–68. Zurich: Lit. Publisher Münster Berlin.

Dixon, Nicholas. 2002. "On Winning and Athletic Superiority." In *Philosophy of Sport: Critical Readings, Crucial Issues*, edited by M. Andrew Holowchak, 220–34. Upper Saddle River: Pearson Education.

———. 2021. "Sport, Meritocracy, and Praise." *Journal of the Philosophy of Sport* 48 (2): 275–92.

Dunlap, Thomas R. 1998. "The Realistic Animal Story: Ernest Thompson Seton, Charles Roberts, and Darwinism." In *The Wild Animal Story*, 237–47. Philadelphia: Temple University Press.

Fender, Brenna. 2018. "Getting Good." *Clean Run* 24 (05): 5.

Fenzi Dog Sports Academy. n.d. Accessed December 8, 2023. https://www.fenzidogsportsacademy.com/.

Fyfe, Diane. 2023. "Introducing Diane Fyfe." In-person interview.

Gillespie, Dair L., Ann Leffler, and Elinor Lerner. 2002. "If It Weren't for My Hobby, I'd Have a Life: Dog Sports, Serious Leisure, and Boundary Negotiations." *Leisure Studies* 21 (3–4): 285–304.

Gillitt, James, and Michelle Gilbert, eds. 2014. *Sport, Animals, and Society*. New York: Routledge.

Hall, Sue. 2023. "Introducing Sue Hall." In-person interview.

Haraway, D. 2003. *The Companion Species Manifesto: Dogs, People, and Significant Otherness*. Chicago: University of Chicago Press.

———. 2008. *When Species Meet*. Minneapolis: University of Minnesota Press.

Hearne, Vicki. 1986. *Adam's Task: Calling Animals by Name*. New York: Alfred A. Knopf.

———. 1994. *Animal Happiness*. New York: HarperCollins.

Henderson, Dion. 1953. *Algonquin: The Story of a Great Dog*. Racine: Western.

Henry, Wayne I. 2013. "Respect and Non-Human Animals." In *Respect: How Do We Get There?*, 99–110. Berlin: Lit. Publisher Münster Berlin.

Holowchak, M. Andrew, ed. 2002. *Philosophy of Sport: Critical Readings, Crucial Issues*. Upper Saddle River: Pearson Education.

Ikonen, Hanna-Mari. 2017. "'I Love My High-Performance Dog': Love for the Sport in Agility Coach

Bibliography

Representations in Social Media." *Sport in Society*, ePrint version, March.

Knight, Kelvin. 2008. "Practices: The Aristotelian Concept." *Analyse & Kritik* 30: 317–29.

Kretchmar, R. Scott. 2019. "Sport as a (Mere) Hobby: In Defense of 'the Gentle Pursuit of a Modest Competence.'" *Journal of the Philosophy of Sport* 46 (3): 367–82.

Kretchmar, Scott. 2015. "Pluralistic Internalism." *Journal of the Philosophy of Sport* 42 (1): 83–100.

LaVaque-Manty, Mika Tapani. 2009. *The Playing Fields of Eton: Equality and Excellence in Modern Meritocracy*. Ann Arbor: University of Michigan Press.

Leopold, Aldo. 1966. *A Sand County Almanac*. New York: Ballantine.

Linzey, Andrew, and Paul Barry Clark, eds. 2004. *Animal Rights: An Historical Anthology*. New York: Columbia University Press.

List, Charles. 2013. *Hunting, Fishing, and Environmental Virtue: Reconnecting Sportsmanship and Conservation*. Corvallis: Oregon State University Press.

Lobel, Arnold. 1980. *Fables*. New York: HarperCollins.

Long, William J. 1998. "The Modern School of Nature-Study and Its Critics." In *The Wild Animal Story*, 144–52. Philadelphia: Temple University Press.

Lowrey, Sassafras. n.d. "History of Dog Agility: The Evolution of the Fast-Paced AKC Sport—American Kennel Club." Accessed December 8, 2023. https://www.akc.org/expert-advice/sports/history-dog-agility-akc-sport/.

Lund, Giuliana. 2014. "Taking Teamwork Seriously: The Sport of Dog Agility as an Ethical Model of Cross-Species Companionship." In *Sport, Animals, and Society*, 101–23. New York: Routledge.

Lutts, Ralph H., ed. 1998. *The Wild Animal Story. Animals, Culture, and Society*. Philadelphia: Temple University Press.

MacIntyre, Alasdair. 1984. *After Virtue*. Second ed. Notre Dame: University of Notre Dame Press.

Magee, Robin. 2023. "Introducing Robin Magee." In-person interview.

Marsal, Eva, Barbara Weber, and Susan T. Gardner, eds. 2013. *Respect: How Do We Get There?* Berlin: Lit. Publisher Münster Berlin.

Meier, Klaus V. 2002. "Triad Trickery: Playing with Sports and Games." In *Philosophy of Sport: Critical Readings, Crucial Issues*, 38–54. Upper Saddle River: Pearson Education.

Moody, Tammy. 2018. "For Play's Sake." *Clean Run* 24 (7): 40–42.

Morris, S.P. 2015. "Moral Luck and the Talent Problem." *Sport, Ethics, and Philosophy* 9 (4): 363–74.

Nagel, Thomas. 1979. *Mortal Questions*. Cambridge: Cambridge University Press.

Nelkin, Dana. 2023. "Moral Luck." In *The Stanford Encyclopedia of Philosophy*, edited by Edward N. Zalta and Uri Nodelman. https://plato.stanford.edu/archives/spr2023/entries/moral-luck.

Nelson, Hilde Lindemann. 2001. *Damaged Identities, Narrative Repair*. Ithaca: Cornell University Press.

Novak, M. 1976. *The Joy of Sports: End Zones, Bases, Baskets, Balls, and the Consecration of the American Spirit*. New York: Basic Books.

Nussbaum, Martha C. 1986. *The Fragility of Goodness: Luck and Ethics in Greek Tragedy and Philosophy*. Cambridge: Cambridge University Press.

Bibliography

Pangman, Jodi, and Ann Benjamin. 2023. "Introducing Jodi Pangman and Ann Benjamin." In-person interview.

Pietricola, Sue. 2023. "Introducing Sue Pietricola." In-person interview.

Ramsay, Hayden. 2005. *Reclaiming Leisure: Art, Sport and Philosophy*. New York: Palgrave Macmillan.

Regan, Tom. 1983. *The Case for Animal Rights*. Berkeley: University of California Press.

Rodi, Robert. 2009. *Dogged Pursuit: My Year of Competing Dusty, the World's Least Likely Agility Dog*. New York: Hudson Street Press.

Russell, R. 1999. "Are Rules All an Umpire Has to Work With?" *Journal of the Philosophy of Sport* 26: 27–49.

———. 2004. "Moral Realism in Sport." *Journal of the Philosophy of Sport* XXXI: 142–60.

Schmid, Steven E. 2014. "Play." In *The Bloomsbury Companion to the Philosophy of Sport*, 366–68. London: Bloomsbury.

Schmid, Walter, T. 2017. *Golf as Meaningful Play: A Philosophical Guide*. Studies in Philosophy of Sport. Lanham: Lexington Books.

Schollmeier, Paul. 1992. "Equine Virtue." *Between the Species* 8(1): 38–43.

Seton, Ernest Thompson. 1901. *Wild Animals I Have Known*. New York: Charles Scribner's Sons.

Shea, Katt, dir. 2022. *Rescued by Ruby*. Netflix.

Simon, R. 2000. "Internalism and Internal Values in Sport (Presidential Address)." *Journal of the Philosophy of Sport* XXVII: 1–16.

Simon, Robert. 2007. "Deserving to Be Lucky: Reflections on the Role of Luck and Desert in Sports." *Journal of the Philosophy of Sport* 34 (1): 13–25.

Stebbins, Robert. 1992. *Amateurs, Professionals, and Serious Leisure*. Montreal: McGill-Queen's University Press.

Strayed, Cheryl. 2012. *Tiny Beautiful Things*. New York: Vintage Books.

Suits, Bernard. 2002. "Tricky Triad: Games, Play, and Sport." In *Philosophy of Sport: Critical Readings, Crucial Issues*, 29–54. Upper Saddle River: Pearson Education.

Sunstein, Cass R., and Martha C. Nussbaum, eds. 2005. *Animal Rights: Current Debates and New Directions*. Oxford: Oxford University Press.

Torres, Cesar R., ed. 2014. *The Bloomsbury Companion to the Philosophy of Sport*. Bloomsbury Companion Series. London: Bloomsbury.

"UK Agility International." n.d. Accessed December 6, 2023. https://ukagilityinternational.com/.

Weber, Ralf. 2019. "Play Is the Way!" Happy Dog Training. February 14. https://happydogtraining.info/advice/play-based-dog-training/.

Weiss, P. 1969. *Sport: A Philosophic Inquiry*. Carbondale: Southern Illinois University Press.

Williams, Bernard. 1981. *Moral Luck: Philosophical Papers 1973–1980*. Cambridge: Cambridge University Press.

Wu, Tim. 2018. "In Praise of Mediocrity." *New York Times Online*, September 29, sec. Opinion.

Xenophon. 1962. *The Art of Horsemanship*. Translated by Morris H. Morgan. London: J.A. Allen.

Yeddo, JoLee. 2023. "Introducing JoLee Yeddo." In-person interview.

Index

Numbers in **bold italics** indicate pages with illustrations.

achievement model of sport 35, 42
agency 2, 29, 50, 64, 94, 128–130, 161
Agility Grand Champion (AGCH) 35, 69
Algonquin 124–125, 144, 170
amateur 6; athletes 14–15, 80; excellence 109, 111, 115, 145; hobbies 27–28, 34, 81–94, 100–101, 104; vs. professionals 71–72, 79; *see also* Booth, Wayne; leisure
American Kennel Club (A.K.C.) 95, **96**, **99**, 168*Ch*5*n*2; courses 36, **37**; lifetime achievement award 13; mission statement 169; organization 28, 34, 105, 114, 120–121; titles 13, 35, 97; trials 4, ***138***, ***143***, ***150***; *see also* Fyfe, Diane
animal happiness 128, 144; *see also* Hearne, Vicki
animal rights 29, 130, 168*ch*6*n*2, 171, 172; *see also* Regan, Tom
Aristotle 3, 11, 167*ch*2*n*8, 169; human flourishing 2, 51–52, 63, 126–127, 144; virtue 127, 167*ch*4*n*2, 168*ch*6*n*1; *see also* external goods
Aussie Acres Agility 29, ***30***, ***33***, 67, 138, 169
Australian Shepherd Club of America (A.S.C.A) 28, 36–39, 41, 105, 114
authentic descriptions of animals 146, 157–158

Bad Dog Agility 27, 67, 167*ch*1*n*3, 167*ch*2*n*4, 169–170
Baier, Annette 132–135, 169
Benjamin, Ann 95–98, **99**, 172
betrayal of trust 132–133
Booth, Wayne 27, 80, 89–91, 104, 169
Boylan, Jennifer Finney 151, 169
Burroughs, John 156, 169

"The Camel Dances" 80–81, 101
Campos, Daniel G. 44, 169
Canine Performance Events (C.P.E.) 26, 28, 34, 36, 38–39, 72, 74–75, 114, 167; *see also* Yeddo, JoLee
Carr, David 52, 167*ch*2*n*6, 169
causal determinism 49–50, 167*ch*2*n*9
cheering 45–47
Clean Run (magazine) 167*ch*1*n*2, 167*ch*2*n*4, 167*ch*3*n*1, 169–171
communication 42–43, 56, 62, 64, 135–137; and ethical excellence 28–29, 34, 108–109, 111, 114, 116, 128, 144; Diane Fyfe 122–123; and respect 128–129; Robin Magee 141–143; Sue Hall 112; *see also* relational values
constitutive luck 49, 56; *see also* luck; moral luck
control 64; Aristotle 51–52; dogs 69–70, 94; human flourishing 2; luck 48–49, 56, 167*ch*2*n*9; training 124, 131, 163–164; trust 134
counterstory 153, 168*ch*7*n*2

Davis, Zach Gulaboff 36–37
Dewey, John 89, 170
Dixon, Nicholas 39–41, 170
Dunlap, Thomas 156, 170

ethical concept of excellence 1, 6, 34, 122, 144; justification for 108
exceptional performance 5; and ethical excellence 9, 17–19, 24–25, 28, 33–57, 70, 77, 85–91, 108–109, 122, 145; and hobbies 92–93
external rewards (goods) 9, 34, 111–112; and agility 114–117, 122, 159; MacIntyre 102–104, 109

Fernandezlopez, Sarah 68, 170
Fyfe, Diane ***110***, 117, ***118***, 119–123, 148–149, 170

games 26, 56, 74–78, 134; and dog play 69; excellence 34, 70–71; golf 62–64;

173

Index

hobbies 87; internal rewards 104, 168*ch*5*n*1; sport 31, 41, 68, 171–172
gestures of trust 135
good life 2, 51, 62, 126; *see also* Aristotle

Hall, Sue 29–*30*, 31–*33*, 112, 124, 170
Haraway, Donna 64, 128, 170
Hearne, Vicki 2, 123, 128, 131–137, 144, 153–154, 170
Henderson, Dion 124–126, 170
Henry, Wayne I. 130, 170
hobby 27–28, 80–100; definition 86–89; excellence 34
human excellence 2, 63, 78; *see also* Aristotle
hybrid virtue 127

ice-cream pleasure 89, 104, 111
Ikonen, Hana-Mari 72, 170
inherent value 130
intellectual virtue 63–64, 70, 127
intelligible behavior 146–147
internal rewards (goods) 9, 28, 102–109, 114, 121, 168*ch*5*n*1

James, William 80

Kretchmar, Scott 14, 18–19, 35, 42–47, 57–66, 87–93, 99, 171

LaVaque-Manty, Mika Tapani 27, 72, 171
leisure 85–86, 91, 99, 109, 145, 167*ch*4*n*2, 170, 172
Leopold, Aldo 86, 99, 171
Lobel, Arnold: "The Camel Dances" 80–81, 100–101, 106, 171
London, Jack 155
Long, William 155, 157–159
luck 39–40, 48–50, 62; *see also* constitutive luck; moral luck
Lund, Giuliana 42–43, 64, 94, 129, 171

MacIntyre, Alasdair 100–108, 114–115, 121, 168*ch*5*n*1, 168*ch*7*n*1, 171; narrative, 145–147, 150–151, 159–160; *see also* external rewards; internal rewards; practice
Magee, Robin 29–*30*, *33*, 67, *126*, 138–143, *138*, *143*, 148, *150*, 171
Moody, Tammy 69, 171
moral character 18–19, 51–52, 56, 62–64, 70, 77, 167*ch*2*n*9
moral luck 49–50, 52, 63, 171–172; *see also* constitutive luck; luck
moral value 18, 35
moral virtue 62–64
Muster Dogs 161–165, 169

Nagel, Thomas 49, 167*ch*2*n*5, 171
narrative 10, 34, 145–160, 166, 170–171; *see also* narrative ethics
narrative ethics 152, 170
nature-faker controversy 153
Nelkin, Dana 49, 171
Novak, Michael 25, 42, 171
Nussbaum, Martha 2, 10, 168*ch*6*n*2, 171–172

Pangman, Jodi 95–99, *96*, 113, 134, 151, 172
paragons of excellence 107
Pietricola, Sue 52–55, *53*, *55*, 112, *155*, 159, 172
play 57–79; primitive 68–71, 78, 91; sophisticated 68–71, 78
practice (MacIntyre) 101–108, 111, 114–115, 121–122
primary intention 146–149, 159
professional 8, 27, 47, 71–72, 79, 89, 172; excellence 90–92, 100
psychological disvalue 18–19, 25, 34–35, 85

recreation 27, 69, 71–72, 79, 81–84; *see also* leisure
Regan, Tom 130, 172
relational values (goods) 9, 28, 107–109, 111, 114, 122, 149, 155, 159–160; *see also* communication; respect; trust
Rescued by Ruby 131–134, 172
respect 24; and ethical excellence 28–29, 34, 108–109, 111–116, 122–123; Robin Magee 139–142; stories 149, 155, 159–166; and training 128–131, 144–145, 170–171; *see also* relational values
responsibility 42–43, 63, 122, 131–136, 161
Roberts, Charles 155, 170
Rodi, Robert 13–19, 62, 172

Schmid, Walter T. 62–63, 172
Schollmeier, Paul 127, 172
serendipitous model of sport 57, 64, 66
Seton, Ernest Thompson 155–156, 170, 172
skills 169; agility 9, 24–27, 44–45, 55, 84, 102–104; development of 9, 30–31, 42, 67, 82, 115–116; and ethical excellence 8, 92, 108, 111, 145; herding 164; hobbies 87–88, 91, 93–95, 100; and play 26, 68–70; and training 136, 139, 144
standards of excellence 26, 28, 34–35, 46–48, 78; practice (MacIntyre) 101–106, 114, 121
stories 10–11, 29, 32, 35, 115, 145–166, 170; Dusty 13–19; ethical value 144,

174

Index

159–161; and excellence 93, explanatory value 152–155; Maggie 19–25, **20**, 57–62; "Muster Dogs" 161–165; *see also* narrative ethics; nature-faker controversy

Strayed, Cheryl 42, 172

subject-of-a-life 130

Suits, Bernard 68–71, 78, 172

teamwork 43, 56, 62–64, 167*ch*2*n*3, 171

training 1, 167*ch*2*n*3, 167*ch*2*n*4, 169–170, 172; communication 64; Dusty 15–16, 94, 98, 112; and ethical excellence 5, 34, 28–29, 93, 106–108, 123–148; exceptional performance 17; hobbies 85–88; Jodi Pangman 113–114; and play 66–70; Robin Magee **138**–144; skills 44–50, 106, 116; Sue Hall 112; Vicki Hearne 123, 128–131, 153; Xenophon 126–127; *see also* "Muster Dogs"

trust 43, 56, 107, 131–135; Diane Fyfe 117, 122; and ethical excellence 28–29, 34, 107–116, 122–123, 128, 144; Jodi Pangman 113–114, 134–135; Robin Magee 139–143; and stories 149, 155, 159–166; Vicki Hearne 136; *see also* relational values

UK Agility International (U.K.I.) 19–21, 25, 38, 111, 134, 172

Weber, Ralf 66–67, 172

Williams, Bernard 49, 172

Wu, Tim 85, 90, 99, 172

Xenophon 127–128, 144, 172

Yeddo, JoLee 26, **65**, 72–77, **73**, **78**, 95, 172

www.ingramcontent.com/pod-product-compliance
Lightning Source LLC
Chambersburg PA
CBHW032047300426
44117CB00009B/1221